THE
FINANCIAL
GOVERNANCE
OF
CHARITIES

TREVOR GAMBLING AND
ROWAN JONES

A report prepared by the Department of
Accounting and Finance,
Birmingham Business School for
the Charities Aid Foundation,
The Institute of Chartered Accountants in
England and Wales, and the Chartered Institute
of Management Accountants

CIMA

The Chartered Institute of
Management Accountants

© CAF ICAEW CIMA

Published by The Charities Aid Foundation
The Institute of Chartered Accountants in England and Wales
The Chartered Institute of Management Accountants

Editor Gillian Clarke
Design and production Eugenie Dodd Typographics
Printed and bound in Great Britain by Bell & Bain Ltd, Glasgow

A catalogue record for this book is available
from the British Library.

ISBN 1–85934–029–6

CAF web address http://www.charitynet.org
ICAEW web page icaew.co.uk

Contents

Foreword

Public attention was focused on corporate governance even before the publication of the Cadbury Report, which suggested that greater efficiency in the management of UK companies could be achieved by the better use of non-executive directors. For registered charities, authority rests with non-executive trustees, so research into charitable governance is part of the ongoing debate. Research published by the Home Office in 1993 suggested that the efforts by trustees to control their charities are often ineffective and result in over-burdensome bureaucracy.

Recent legislation has strengthened the accounting disclosure and auditing requirements for charities but, as the authors of this report point out, accounting systems are only as good as the administrative systems that support them. Given that very little is known about the administrative procedures of charities, especially descriptions of what actually occurs, it becomes apparent that this is an under-researched area.

The work done by the research team has generated a rich set of data and provides insight into a wide range of charitable structures. Scholarly, without being inaccessible, this report concludes with a list of well thought out recommendations.

This book marks the first joint venture between two leading accountancy institutes, The Institute of Chartered Accountants in England and Wales (ICAEW) and the Chartered Institute of Management Accountants (CIMA), and the Charities Aid Foundation (CAF). For the first time, CIMA and ICAEW jointly funded a project; half the funds were contributed from CIMA's research budget and half from charitable funds associated with the ICAEW. CAF made a valuable contribution by arranging access to the eighteen charities examined and by bearing the costs of publishing the report.

Judy Stammers   David Hunt
Chairman   *Chairman*
CIMA Research and   *ICAEW Research Board*
Technical Committee

Preface

We are accountants whose research in the charitable sector has been concerned with the development of Statements of Recommended (Accounting) Practice. One major conclusion we reached was that the annual reports and accounts, upon which so many of the recent reforms concentrate, can only be as good as the administrative systems that underpin them. Moreover, whilst there has been much controversy surrounding charities – including significant pieces of published research – we could find no modern literature that described, much less theorised about, these administrative systems. Indeed, the situation was no different from that faced by, for example, the Cadbury Committee on the Financial Aspects of Corporate Governance, which deals with public companies. This report of our research describes the administrative systems of eighteen charities; they have different characteristics, which makes it possible to offer generalisations about the charitable sector. Nevertheless, it is not appropriate for a report such as this to attempt to construct a general theory of the financial management of charities; such theorising will emerge later. Instead, we raise issues for further discussion; we hope they help in that discussion.

Acknowledgements

Thanks are due to the trustees and managers of our eighteen case studies and to four anonymous referees; we also acknowledge the help of DePaul University, Chicago, and the University of Illinois at Chicago in providing office support during the writing of this report.

Although this is our research report to the Charities Aid Foundation, The Institute of Chartered Accountants in England and Wales, and the Chartered Institute of Management Accountants, none of these bodies necessarily shares the views expressed, which are ours alone.

Summary of the report

Chapter 1

This report synthesises the administrative procedures of eighteen charities. It might be of interest for its own sake or as a contribution to the current concern about 'corporate governance' in general. However, these procedures are especially important for a charity because a proper understanding of its affairs requires a full and credible narrative report. This credibility depends on the transparency of the administrative machinery from which the narrative emerges.

Chapter 2

The eighteen charities are a mixture of larger and smaller charities, some of which operate at local level, others at national level, some at international level, and some at all three. The sample includes organisations, such as an NHS healthcare trust and a university, that could have been exempted from registration. Senior paid officials and trustees were interviewed in the course of the study.

Chapter 3

Most of the charities examined here have 'members' and/or 'branches' but there appear to be considerable differences over their status and the formal arrangements, if any, by which they make their views known to the administration. The issues we raise for discussion are:

3a whether all members of a charity should have the right to receive copies of the annual report and accounts, attend an AGM and vote thereat;

3b whether the AGM should have powers to elect non-executive trustees and other officers, to reappoint the auditors and to receive the annual report and accounts;

3c whether the Chair at such AGMs should be taken by an appointed or elected president, who is not a trustee;

3d whether charities should draw up the regulations relating to branches so as to make it clear to what extent, if at all, branches or regions can act in an autonomous fashion;

3e whether the remits of regional paid officials should be drawn up in a precise manner, so as to determine their responsibilities and authority both to the branches etc and to the charity as a whole.

Chapter 4

Proper governance seems to require a charity to formulate a policy within the terms of its constitution and then to execute it. The formulation of policy may require quite a large deliberative assembly to ensure that all relevant views and possibilities for action are properly aired; executive action is difficult except through a small group of people. The issues we raise for discussion are:

4a whether a charity should establish a council whose primary purpose is the setting of policy;

4b whether this council should be large enough to provide representation for all the regional and sectional interests that have relevance to its objects;

4c whether the membership of other, purely executive, committees should number between three and twelve;

4d whether trustees should continue to serve beyond the age of 70, or for longer than (say) six years without a break.

Chapter 5

There are considerable *de jure* differences between the procedures through which the charities select and appoint their trustees. *De facto* the differences are less marked. The difficulty of finding people willing to devote the necessary time tends to turn many boards of trustees into self-perpetuating oligarchies. When this is not the case, the contrary danger is that well-organised extremists may attempt to take over the charity. In the present climate of opinion, the election of trustees should be conducted on democratic principles but it is essential that the results of polls truly represent the views of all concerned. The issues we raise for discussion are:

5a whether charities should draft their regulations with respect to membership with especial care so as to ensure that only bona fide supporters of their aims can be admitted, or retain membership;

5b whether charities should grant 'membership status' to all such supporters who assist with their work in a regular and substantial fashion over a suitable period of time;

5c whether candidates for the office of non-executive trustee should be nominated by the membership;

5d whether, if a charity has branches, votes for elections to national office should be made by those attending branch AGMs, wherever possible;

5e whether, unless the membership is substantially local in nature, any charity-wide elections to national office should be by postal ballot;

5f whether proxy-voting should be discouraged.

Chapter 6

A curious finding in our research is the diversity of titles by which trustees are known. Moreover, the large size of some boards of trustees suggests that it is unlikely that all members can truly act as charitable trustees, within the meaning of charity law; at the same time, there are other groups, principally the senior paid officials of these charities, who might well be carrying out all the duties of such trustees. The issues we raise for discussion are:

6a whether all trustees should include the word 'trustee' in their title;

6b whether the existence of classes of executive trustees and non-executive trustees should be recognised;

6c whether the number of non-executive trustees should be at least equal to that of the executive trustees, plus one, and their Chair should be drawn from among them;

6d whether it should be recognised that executive trustees can be employees of their charities, and remunerated accordingly, but that no payments should normally be made to non-executive trustees (except for out-of-pocket expenses);

6e whether appropriate fees may be paid to non-executive trustees who act for the charity in a professional capacity, which may include the detailed inspection and supervision of the activities of executive employees of the charity;

6f whether, wherever salaries or fees of any sort are payable to any trustees, the charity should set up a remuneration committee, consisting of uninvolved non-executive trustees, or designate some substantial outside person or agency to monitor the amounts so paid;

6g   whether the word 'trustee' should not be used in the title of any person who is not a trustee within the meaning of the Charities Act. The sole exception would be the use of the title 'honorary trustee' in cases where the person so named has no part whatsoever in the administration of the charity; in this regard, we suggest that the title 'life trustee' may be particularly misleading;

6h   whether it should be possible to appoint persons (who might be called 'vice presidents') to represent the charity at a senior level, who take no part in its administration and are therefore not trustees;

6i   whether it should be possible for other bodies or offices to nominate persons (who might be called 'institutional representatives') to be their representatives in the charity, without taking any part in its administration;

6j   whether it should be possible for the council of a charity to comprise both classes of representative, together with the executive and non-executive trustees of the charity;

6k   whether it should be possible for non-trustee members of council to take full part in the discussion of matters of policy, and other administrative matters such as the approval of the annual report and accounts;

6l   whether voting rights on council should be reserved to the trustees;

6m   whether all the members of any standing committee of the charity should be listed under an appropriate category in the 'legal and administrative information' section of the annual report; and

6n   whether members of such committees who are not otherwise listed as 'trustees' or 'principal officers' should be listed and described as 'senior executive volunteers'.

Chapter 7

An earlier study by the National Council of Voluntary Organisations (NCVO, 1992) suggested that many trustees were not well versed in their responsibilities and some were unaware that their position in the charity was actually that of a trustee. Our research revealed no examples of total ignorance, perhaps because we tended to interview the more senior trustees. Nevertheless, a considerable diversity of views seems to exist about their roles and particularly over the extent to which a trustee may rely on other parties. The issues we raise for discussion are:

7a whether charities should take steps to ensure that all candidates for trusteeship fully understand the nature of the duties and responsibilities they have offered to undertake;

7b whether charities should provide some formal induction process to consolidate this understanding in newly appointed trustees;

7c whether these processes should be seen by both the charity and the trustee as the first step in an on-going process of continuing education in charity matters;

7d whether suitable instruction in relevant aspects of charity law and procedures should be given to all voluntary workers, especially those with executive or fundraising responsibilities;

7e whether participation in all these educational opportunities (or a parallel programme) should be mandatory for any members of the paid staff of the charity who play any part in its administrative processes;

7f whether charities should ensure, as far as possible, that their professional advisers and their staffs have also engaged in suitable courses of professional education on charity matters.

Chapter 8

Another matter of diversity was in the names given to the various committees and subcommittees of the charities. Obviously, the important thing is that the trustees themselves understand the remits of their committees. On the other hand, outside bodies and the ordinary members of a charity might be misled by some of the nomenclature in use. The issues we raise for discussion are:

8a whether any meeting comprising the whole body of trustees, but excluding any non-trustees, should be called 'the Board of Trustees';

8b whether the title 'Council' should be confined to committees comprising both trustees and representatives;

8c whether the title 'executive committee' be reserved for a committee that consists solely of paid and unpaid executive trustees;

8d whether a committee comprising the Chair of the charity and the chairs of its subcommittees should be known as 'the committee of chairs';

8e whether a committee that consolidates materials on behalf of the council might simply be referred to as 'the sub-council';

8f whether the title of every committee should clearly indicate the nature of its remit;

8g whether purely advisory committees should include that word in their titles;

8h whether any words added to the title 'finance committee' should clearly indicate the scope of its remit.

Chapter 9

A small but important issue emerged over the servicing of these committees. Many chief executives and/or their deputies attend almost every meeting of every committee, and often service them in person or through their own secretary. This may be appropriate in some cases but, when the chief executive has a definite managerial role, the resulting burden on that officer can be very great. The issue we raise for discussion is:

9a whether, where a charity has a considerable number of committees to be serviced, a reasonably senior 'committee clerk' should be appointed for the purpose.

Chapter 10

Finally, we consider those aspects of financial governance that have become more familiar as a result of the Cadbury Report: audit committees, appointment committees, salaries and remuneration committees. Allied to these issues are systems of budgetary control, management accounting and internal control generally, together with the important issue of reserve policy. The issues we raise for discussion are:

10a whether a charity should always have an audit committee, consisting of all of the non-executive trustees;

10b whether that committee should meet at least twice a year, with the external auditor in attendance, but with no other trustees or paid officials present, except for a minute-secretary;

10c whether one meeting should consider the various compliance reports on the charity's system, and establish the auditor's programme of work in the light of these reports;

10d whether the audit committee should meet on another occasion to consider the audited accounts, together with a detailed analysis of any adjustments made to the cumulative management accounts, and the auditor's 'management letter' or other commentary on the audit or the accounts, prior to their submission to the board or council for approval;

10e whether, at least once in every three years, the committee should consider the detail of the charity's financial control systems, and invite the auditor's comments thereon;

10f whether, at least once in every three years, the committee ought to reconsider the terms of the auditor's letter of engagement;

10g whether every charity should prepare at least an annual budget, which should be approved by the full Board of Trustees;

10h whether, at least once a quarter, all members of the Board of Trustees should receive a set of cumulative management accounts, setting out variances with the budget, and proper minutes should be kept of any comments thereon and the explanations put forward to explain any variances;

10i whether every charity should prepare a formal trustees' report, on behalf of the whole Board of Trustees, that complies fully with the spirit of the Charities Statement of Recommended Practice (SORP);

10j whether the audit committee should formally consider the adequacy of this report, in the light of the minutes of the Board of Trustees, before its submission to the board or council for approval;

10k whether the professional bodies of accountants should be urged to include more material on both voluntary sector accounting and auditing *and* communication skills in their examination syllabuses and requirements for practical experience;

10l whether charities should expend the whole of their income every year, subject to making provision for known long-term liabilities and any properly calculated reserves for the future;

10m whether charities should adopt the technique of flexible budgeting and whether such a budget should always underlie any reserves of funds to be carried forward;

10n whether any such reserves should be set aside into a designated contingency fund.

Broad conclusions

Over all, our research leads us to believe that the voluntary sector has reached a level of development at which the current, cumulative, legal and fiscal arrangements can be made to conform to the reality of their situations only by the most complex administrative machinery. It is possible that it is these complexities that give rise to apparently excessive regulation of the voluntary sector and excessive complications in the tax regime.

We hope that the effect of this research project and of an ever-increasing body of studies in this area will be a major and fundamental reform of the whole corpus of legislation relating to voluntary organisations.

In our view the goal should be the possibility of registering an incorporate voluntary organisation with limited liability and the right to trade (along the lines of the proposals relating to the European Association), together with a tax regime driven by a specific social policy toward such organisations.

CHAPTER ONE

Introduction

The primary purpose of the research on which this report is based was to understand how charities are actually governed. Our emphasis was on financial governance, including budgetary control; however, because of the obvious difficulties in demonstrating the efficiency and effectiveness of charitable expenditures, we also examined the control exercised by trustees over the charitable operations.

Forms of administration

The law relating to charities has little, and has always had little, to say about how a charity should be organised. In the context of the welfare state, this would accord with the view that the voluntary sector has existed primarily to fill in the gaps left by the 'official' provisions for the welfare of citizens. Thus charitable activity has commonly had to devise new forms of provision, and these in turn may have required new forms of administration. Our study might have been justified merely by recording the wide variety of charitable governance to be found in the United Kingdom at the present time – indeed, although limited to eighteen charities, it does this.

But it also seems appropriate to enquire whether those forms of administration are truly appropriate to the present operations of the charities in question. Administrative reform is rarely popular with those who enjoy authority under a different regime and, in any case, many charities feel it a mark of efficiency to devote the smallest possible resources to administrative matters. Consequently, it seems possible that there are some charities whose administrative procedures reflect either an earlier pattern of charitable provision or earlier ideas of what constitutes 'good administrative practice' – or both.

Financial governance

Moreover, the financial governance of charities has become a more general issue for public concern. Some of this concern is just part of the more general unease that led to the Cadbury Report on the Financial Aspects of Corporate Governance. But probably even more significantly there have been a number of scandals relating to charities themselves. These in part led to the Charities Acts of 1992 and 1993, which in turn have stimulated a newly revised Statement of Recommended Practice (SORP) setting out specific recommendations for 'Accounting by Charities', and Home Office regulations on the same topic. These Acts represent radical reform to a sector that is notoriously difficult to rationalise: charities derive from a long history of incremental, piecemeal consideration. The fundamental question of their taxation has become ever more complex as taxation itself has; other heterogeneous forms of regulation that depend on the particular kind of charity, as well as the changing role of the Charity Commission, have similarly been added in something of an ad hoc way. The time does indeed seem right for a fundamental review.

Accountability

An essential problem with recent reform is that much of it is predicated on the notion that more and better financial disclosure will provide sufficient 'transparency' to resolve any problems arising from the dealings of either company directors or charitable trustees – by making what was going on obvious to all concerned. Unfortunately, this is not always so. Many modern organisations are seen to be no longer truly 'accountable'. At a superficial level, this is because of the development of complex capital structures whose ambiguous nature is reflected in ambiguous accounting: this can be regulated (but hardly corrected) by accounting standards. At a rather deeper level, one must question the validity of the accounting numbers and transactions themselves, to the extent that forceful and morally indifferent people are able to seize control of organisations and operate them as their private fiefdoms – and ensure that the accounting record does not disclose this fact. At the deepest level, however, one must question what any accounts mean – in the absence of our own assumptions about their significance.

The accounts of a trading organisation seem to have significance, if we care to assume that it is operating in a reasonably efficient market. If its income exceeds the costs of providing the goods and services it produces, we assume it is adding value by what it does. If the net profit be compared with the value of the capital invested in the business, we assume that this reflects the efficiency with which the firm's capital is being employed. Moreover, if we can be assured that the assets and liabilities are fairly stated, these measures of the added value and efficiency are not directly affected by the possibility that the directors or others may have been guilty of unfair trading or embezzlement: if the returns are adequate, we will be satisfied.

Without these assumptions, the accounts are no more than listings of income and expenditure – and no such assumptions can be made of a charity, or indeed of any not-for-profit organisation. Even for a trading organisation, the assumptions may not be true: markets are not very efficient, and may not reflect the true social costs (and benefits) of the operation. In short, of themselves the accounting records tell the reader nothing at all about the *qualitative* aspects of the transactions they report.

This is why we need to know more about any organisation than can possibly be reported through its accounts. The qualitative shortfall in our understanding can be made good by a narrative report and supplementary statistical information. But this type of reporting lacks the systematic coherence of the accounting record: how can we be sure that the narrative is a comprehensive summary of everything that has happened? Might it not be supplying a partial, anecdotal picture of the situation – whether by omission or by design? More generally, is it possible to audit a narrative?

It is possible to audit such a report, but only in circumstances similar to those that make it possible to audit an accounting statement. A small trader may simply hand a bundle of vouchers and till-rolls over to an accountant and expect the latter to produce some accounts. This is entirely possible, but they cannot be audited unless they fit into a *system* of cashbooks and ledger accounts which at least provide some grounds for belief that the record is *complete*. In the same way, one can be assured that a narrative report is complete only if it emerges from an *administrative* system that provides grounds for believing that the *qualitative* aspects of all the organisation's transactions must have passed through the appropriate channels and been properly recorded as they did so.

Summary

In summary, any assurance as to the adequacy of what a charity says about itself, whether in the form of accounts or narrative, depends on the quality of its administrative system. The focus of the changes in the new Charities Acts and the Charities SORP relating to financial matters is on 'improvements' to the reports and accounts of charities. Our purpose here is to report on the underlying administrative systems, which are not for the most part addressed by these regulations. And our basic proposition is that a fundamental review of these systems, with the likelihood of significant change to them, is necessary if the changes relating to charity reports and accounts are to be meaningful.

CHAPTER TWO

The subjects of the study

We investigated the administrative systems of eighteen charities from across the charitable sector, by interviewing the chief executive (or another member of the senior management team) of each, as well as some of their trustees. All our respondents are registered charities, although they include a number that might, had they wished, have been exempted from registration.

The charities

Throughout this report the charities are anonymous: we have numbered them from 1 to 18. However, in order to provide some context, we give the following brief descriptions:

Charity number	Brief description
1	An NHS healthcare trust, which operates a regional hospital servicing two smallish towns and some rural areas on the fringe of a major conurbation. It is not a particularly large hospital, as regional hospitals go, but is clearly a relatively large organisation compared with most local charities.
2	A local community association operating within a community school in a major industrial conurbation. It is quite the smallest charity in our sample.
3	A national charity serving the needs and interests of sufferers from a specific medical condition and of those who care for them. It does not directly fund medical research. The charity may be considered to be fairly large.
4	A charity concerned with animal welfare of a specific nature, which operates in the UK and the Republic of Ireland. It comprises a number of affiliated organisations and may be considered to be a large charity.
5	A long-established local housing association. Given its capital-intensive nature, it may be considered to be a large charity by local standards; however, it is not particularly large as housing associations go.
6	A specialist umbrella organisation that acts principally as an intermediary between a large number of charities and donors. A large national charity.

7	An umbrella organisation, albeit one that is less specialised than Charity 6, which assists member-charities with a variety of organisational, legal and financial problems. It is a national organisation but not a particularly large one.
8	A housing association, much more recently established than Charity 5, operating in a major conurbation. Given its capital-intensive nature, it may be considered to be a large charity by local standards; however, it is not particularly large as housing associations go.
9	A major national charity concerned with the national heritage. It is a very large charity indeed.
10	A national foundation that makes grants for a variety of charitable purposes and funds many in-house projects. It is a substantial organisation, although not particularly large in comparison with some other grant-making foundations.
11	A comparatively small local charity concerned with the welfare of sufferers from a specific disease and with those who care for them.
12	This major charity operates throughout the UK and the Republic of Ireland. It promotes assistance for a particular class of catastrophe. Especially in view of its massive capital equipment needs, it may be considered a very substantial charity.
13	A major national charity concerned with a broad spectrum of animal welfare activities. It may be considered to be a very large charity.
14	An international charity providing assistance in catastrophic situations; a very large charity indeed.
15	A charity concerned with education and preservation of the national heritage. Although its appeal is to a national and international audience, it may be said to be a medium-sized local charity.
16	A charity concerned with the welfare of a particular class of British citizen at home and overseas. It functions mostly as an enabling charity that provides the trained volunteer force to assist its clients, largely relying on other agencies to provide the funding. It may be considered to be a fairly large national charity.
17	A 'new' university and one of the largest non-collegiate universities in the UK.
18	A national federation of independent schools. It can be described as a conglomerate of medium-sized local charities. The overall federation is rather small compared with many national charities.

The interviews

The initial interview was with the chief executive of the charity, or some other member of the senior management team. This took the form of a structured interview. This structure was provided by a checklist (reproduced as an Appendix to this report) which was loosely based on an early draft of a questionnaire produced by a committee concerned to establish an 'Accreditation Bureau for Charities', of which one of the authors is a member.

To complement our interviews with senior management, we also sought interviews with one or more of the trustees themselves. We were able to establish communication with sixteen of them, and spoke to each for about an hour. Although we had prepared a checklist for these interviews, they were, by design, structured less formally than those we had previously had with the paid officials. It was not our intention to verify what we had been told in the previous interview; rather our aim was to hear from each trustee how they went about exercising 'the general control, responsibility and management of the administration' of their charities. Although we refer to our trustee respondents as 'Trustee A' through to 'Trustee P', these letters do not correspond with the numbers we have assigned to the charities; they are not even placed in the same order.

Following the interviews with senior management and the trustees, the interviewer produced a written record of the meeting. This record was subsequently sent to all interviewees for their approval. In all cases except two, approval was given; in the two exceptions, no response was received. The quotations in the body of this report are from the written record of the interviews.

These respondents do not represent a random sample of the trustees of our sample of charities. They were the people suggested by the paid officials whom we had interviewed on the first occasion. This was probably unavoidable, as there seemed comparatively little enthusiasm among the trustees at large to be interviewed, possibly because of the considerable demands that trusteeship makes on the spare time of those who volunteer to serve in this way. Our interviewees tended to be among those who were required to do something or other for their charities, on a more or less weekly basis, and our sample is therefore heavily biased toward senior trustees, and indeed toward office-holders – chairs and treasurers. In particular, they include only one 'representative' or '*ex officio*' trustee, who was also in fact the Chair of his charity.

The issues

With a view to setting the scene for the more detailed material, the following three issues relating to each of our subjects were determined at the outset:

- the extent of governmental funding;
- the practices for reviewing cost-effectiveness and administrative controls;
- whether the charity had a formal 'mission statement'.

Governmental funding

The extent of governmental funding of the charities ranged from 100% to nil – and included a 'don't know' – but the response commonly revealed some basic facts about each charity's operations, as opposed to its governance. 'Government money' tends to be ring-fenced, even when it is given as core-funding.

Thus the NHS healthcare trust is almost 100% government funded. However, these funds reach the hospital through the budgets of the various 'fundholders' of the 'internal market' for health services whose patients are treated by the hospital. The tiny non-government element is not without interest: this comprises a number of comparatively small 'ward funds' and similar benefactions, which are currently held by the Area Health Authority on behalf of the trust, but are likely to be transferred to the hospital in due course:

'The Chief Executive observes that while these items are not very significant in this case, "ward funds" etc of this type are a very substantial source of funds in many older-established hospitals, especially if they are well known for some "popular" specialism.'

Again, the different levels of funding from the Housing Association reveal essential differences between our two housing associations. The one that is more recently established – and traditional in its activities – receives nearly half of its income from this source; the other is much older and receives only 6% from this source. This reflects a much larger fully funded housing stock in the latter charity – and also the fact that it has rather wider objects of social and aesthetic engineering.

The community centre was set up by the local authority as part of a community-school initiative 'very much in accordance with the ideas of the 1970s', and receives about 60% of its core-funding from it. One of our umbrella charities is in fact the 'umbrella' for this community centre; this too receives about 60% of its funds from (in this case) central government. Most of this is core-funding from the Voluntary Service Unit but some comes from specific contract work for the Department for Education and Employment (DfEE).

The other umbrella organisation reports some minor funding from both the British government and the European Union. One of the 'catastrophe' charities has no state funding beyond a nominal £100,000 donation from the Republic of Ireland, in recognition of its continued service in that country. The other such charity is a major international force, which receives about 50% of its income in the form of grants from several governments – including that of the UK.

The welfare-enabling charity receives no core-funding from the British government, although its beneficiaries are the families of a particular group of government employees. Nevertheless, about 50% of the charity's total income comes from the appropriate government department, to pay for the provision of maternity, health visitor and social worker services in areas (mainly overseas) where these are deficient. This income 'has not been segregated into a trading company, but treated as a part of the income of the Services Support Department. The current "market testing" exercise by government departments has resulted in a considerable broadening of the terms of the proposed future . . . contract, to include [other] beneficiaries, so the desirability of hiving down this work to a trading company is under review.'

Some 10–14% of the income of one of our 'heritage' charities is in the form of non-core-funding from government sources. The other receives nothing from this source at present, but observes that English Heritage might be a source of future funding in appropriate circumstances. This is also the case with our educational charity, because a number of its schools are at least partially housed in ancient buildings of architectural or historical importance. The university receives about 90% of its income from student and residential grants.

These last two charities raise an interesting point with respect to the extent of 'government funding'. The university's core-funding is calculated on its relevant student numbers; this is not the case with the independent schools, although a fair number of their pupils are beneficiaries under the Assisted Places Scheme. Another point of interest is that our respondent at the schools did not know the proportion of the charity's total income coming from this scheme. He knew what it was for 'his' schools, but he had no knowledge of the position at the others – something that first alerted us to the fact that this charity was of a 'federal' nature.

In the same way, one of our housing associations reported that:

'[new] housing policies are producing a very different type of tenant from those originally housed on the estates; almost all newcomers are on supplementary welfare benefits. The result is a need for the Trust to provide many more "social service" and "educational" facilities than in the past.'

Both the Assisted Places Scheme and housing benefit result in payments being made directly to these charities from the government, without the bother and occasional doubt of collecting them from the beneficiaries or their guardians – and produce tenants and pupils who might not otherwise be there at all. Of course, most charities also receive 'government money' in the form of tax refunds on dividends and covenants.

Cost-effectiveness and administration

Another general enquiry as to the practices for reviewing cost-effectiveness and administrative controls revealed a closely related point of interest. Local or central government funding on any notable scale commonly produces a corresponding governmental or quasi-governmental inspection. Thus the audit of the NHS trust is carried out by the District Auditor, and therefore covers general efficiency and compliance, in addition to the purely financial 'external audit'. A return must also be made to the District Health Authority. The District Auditor is also concerned with the activities of the community association, in addition to an annual external audit. In part this may reflect the closeness of the ties to the local authority, which is demonstrated also by the fact that this charity's paid officials are all seconded local government officers; moreover, there is also a check on the quarterly return that the association is required to make to the local authority about its activities.

The university is subject to inspections by both the Higher Education Funding Council for England (HEFCE) and the Higher Education Quality Council (HEQC), whilst the housing associations are visited once every three or four years by inspectors from the Housing Corporation. One umbrella charity has a triennial review by the Voluntary Service Unit, plus an annual review by the DfEE in respect of the work it does for the latter. The other umbrella charity operates what are in effect a bank and an investment trust for other charities; this renders it liable to regulation by the Bank of England, a process that involves a special Banking Act report from a firm of auditors who specialise in bank audits. The schools are subject to the Independent Schools Inspectorate, while any boarding establishments are regularly visited by the local Social Services departments. The welfare-enabling charity is also subject to local authority inspection of the hostels etc that it operates, and also with respect to an (overseas) adoption agency.

Six respondents reported that they have an internal audit section, while (a not entirely identical) six referred to ad hoc reviews by trustees or external consultants; at least two of these seem to have been full-blown 'Working Practices Reviews', inspired by similar exercises in civil service departments. Yet another six reported no internal audit or other specific exercise on general efficiency, but what one of them said on this point may be of interest:

'. . . there is no internal audit section; it is thought that the operation is not sufficiently large to warrant one. Moreover, the Foundation's activities have a certain stability, which makes it possible to control them effectively by other means. Its administrative costs are, of course, reviewed continually, and it is proposed to develop some system for evaluating the effectiveness of grants made.'

The welfare-enabling charity also commented on the apparently curious fact that the government department responsible for their very large grant does not undertake any general inspection of the operations it finances (although detailed reports are, of course, demanded).

'This may be explained by the fact that the provision of care by the charity is closely associated with the command structures of the units being served. Local commanders at home and overseas pay considerable attention to what is being provided, and demand explanations of any perceived inadequacies. Unlike other "benevolent" charities, the beneficiaries in this case have active and influential advocates.'

Mission statement

Whether the charity had a formal 'mission statement' was another introductory enquiry we made of our case studies. The Charities SORP attaches considerable importance to the presentation of such a statement, because, in the absence of some generally accepted assumptions about how charities operate, their annual reports only begin to take on meaning if they can be reviewed in the light of the objectives the charity has set itself. A couple of our respondents did refer to this need to conform to the SORP, but in fact all our respondents except three appear to have a specifically drawn-up formal statement about their mission. Two of those that do not simply refer enquirers respectively to their Charter and to the Special Act of Parliament, but the third was more forthright:

'The "Guide to Applicants", sent to those seeking grants, sets out the Foundation's fields of interest. More generally, the trustees are of the opinion that orotund statements of general principle can be a waste of time, and indeed an excuse for inactivity.'

Seven respondent charities include the statement as a part of a business plan or strategic plan. It is possible that the need to produce such plans to the satisfaction of governmental and other grant-makers has brought about this useful development.

Financing an organisation

Finally, we need to be aware that there are two very different ways of financing an organisation, and the method in use will dictate a good deal of its administrative machinery. Some organisations are essentially 'self-financing', in that they generate all the income needed to support their activities from the sale of their *charitable* products or services, or at least sufficient to maintain their current level of activity. Such organisations may well seek donations and grants to expand their activity, much as a commercial venture will raise additional capital for the same purpose. Charities 1, 5, 6, 15, 17 and 18 fall into this category. They are truly 'not-for-profit' businesses. Charity 10 is also self-financing, in another fashion; it finances its activities from its own endowments, as 'foundations' commonly do.

By contrast, the remaining charities do not have anything like so direct a link between their charitable expenditure and the income needed to finance it. They have to undertake specific 'fundraising activity', and budget their operations within their expected income from appeals, grants, subscriptions, legacies, the covenanted income from trading companies and the like. For that reason they might be described as 'budget-financing organisations', because they use their budgets in essentially the same way that public sector organisations financed by taxes do: as a periodic request for money. Many such charities have some self-financing features: in addition to the fairly general use of trading companies as a source of income, two of our otherwise budget-financing respondents provide certain types of service in return for charges that cover the cost of providing them. However, it is very rare to find any organisation that cannot be confidently assigned to one financial category or another. It is important for a charity to decide the category in which it belongs. The principal method of raising finance has a profound influence on the committee structure and on methods of selecting the trustees of a charity.

The remainder of this report covers the important findings of the research. Each chapter includes data, usually in the form of one or more tables that are expanded mainly using quotations from the transcripts of the interviews with the managers and the trustees. Then some analysis follows, including a number of discussion points presented in shaded boxes.

CHAPTER THREE

Branches and members

Two of the most tenuous concepts in the voluntary sector are those of 'a branch' and 'a member'. A parallel issue is that of 'related charities', although charities often seem unhappy to recognise an ongoing relationship with any other organisation, let alone account for them in any way. These facts can be the cause of misunderstanding, especially compared with commercial companies, where questions of who is or is not a shareholder, or whether some entity is a subsidiary or an associate, a branch office or branch factory, are mostly unambiguous.

Branches

Table 1 shows briefly the numbers of branches and members (and other 'people' statistics) in our respondent charities, but the discussion that follows will illustrate the range of meaning to be found behind these concepts.

Some charities are rather exclusive, and many organisations that seem to be an integral part of their activities will turn out to be quite independent. Others seem to be such 'broad churches' that almost any organisation that gives a nod toward their objects becomes some sort of a branch. Thus:

'There is a "League of Friends" of the hospital, but it is an autonomous charity, in no way accountable to the trust for its activities.'

'The charity has no branches as such. However, it has about fourteen in-house "sections" (such as mothers and toddlers), with their own committees, and whose small funds are kept as part of those of the charity. In addition, there are about ten "affiliated organisations", who simply "hire the facilities" although they are required to conform to the rules of the association in various respects.'

'During 1993 membership continued to rise. On 1 December 1993 [the charity] had 60,656 members, which included 18,621 members of one or more of the major disciplines . . . In addition, [a related organisation] had 38,000 members and [an "affiliated" organisation] represented approximately 43,000 members.' [Taken from the charity's Members' Yearbook]

'The charity has a branch in Moscow, and is considering establishing one in Brussels; these branches are not autonomous. There is a further organisation, which is registered as a charitable company in the USA. It is autonomous and does not operate as any sort of subsidiary of the main charity. However, it receives grants from the main charity, and has many links with it – including the fact that its accounts are prepared by the main charity's Finance Department. Its annual accounts are audited by an associate of the charity's UK auditors . . . There are bi-monthly International Division meetings in London, at which full reports of activities are given by the relevant directors and line-managers.'

'The charity has dealings with 22 semi-autonomous "local federal organisations", which are regional groupings of member organisations, separately registered as charities but operating under an annual agreement

TABLE 1 PEOPLE IN CHARITIES

Charity	Number of branches	Number of members	Is there an AGM?	Number of volunteers	Number of part-time staff	Number of full-time staff	Number of senior staff	Any thefts?
1	0	?	Yes	0	0	1,400	5	0
2	0	?	Yes	5+	35	3	3	0
3	603	67,000	Company	7,000	0	240	7	3 small
4	Innumerable	62,000+	Company	A lot	0	90	12	0
5	0	0	No	0	0	150	9	0
6	2	0	Yes	10	20	160	5	0
7	22	825	Company	5	3	6	4	0
8	0	322	Company	0	200	335	10	0
9	200	2.4 million	Yes	28,000	3,000	3,000	9	1
10	0	0	No	6	13	17	4	0
11	0	2?	Company?	120	5	4	4	0
12	2,000+	30,000+	Yes	5,000+	0	740	9	2 small
13	200	20,000+	Yes	20,000	450	850	9	1
14	800	Trustees	Company	17,000	0	5,500	8	0
15	0?	0	No	A few	130–150	90	3	0
16	1,000	7,520	Yes	7,000?	0	295	11	2
17	0?	Trustees	Company	0	383	1,590	23	2?
18	4	Trustees	Yes	0	3	2,400	3	0

? not clear from interview

with the charity, setting out rights and obligations on both sides. They are all required to adopt a model constitution. Most of these federal organisations do not engage in large-scale local fundraising, as such, although some do receive support in cash or in kind from their local authority. Member organisations pay their subscriptions to the charity, although in some local federal organisations (LFOs), they are collected by the LFO on the charity's behalf. The LFO receives a rebate of part of the membership fee paid by its member organisations.'

'The charity has 200 branches, but these are seen as "associations" in no way under the control of the charity. All members of the charity may become members of their local association. They are analogous to the "League of Friends" of a hospital, but they are not registered charities in their own right. Neither are they solely concerned with raising funds for the charity; in general they have their own agenda of interests, which are parallel to but not part of the work of the charity. The regional offices of the charity maintain contact with the associations in their areas, but do not control them.'

'The charity has no branches as such. However, it has a substantial in-house research/development project operating from another location, which has many features of a branch activity.'

'There is a "support group" [in a neighbouring town], which collects and remits funds . . . This "group" has its own bank account, but its transactions and balances are not included in the charity's own accounts.'

'The charity has no branches, although it is interesting . . . that the Charity Commissioners have registered two quite tiny endowments as special funds. This may be because of the statutory constitution of the main charity. There are a number of ancillary activities associated with the objects of the Trust, going on in and around the charity's premises, which might be seen as non-autonomous or even autonomous branches.'

'The university has no branches, in the sense of affiliated colleges etc. However, the Students' Union operates as a branch of the charity in most respects.'

'The [unincorporated] charity operates through five regional companies which are both limited companies and autonomous charities in their own right . . . There are also 24 schools attached to the appropriate regional companies. These each have a School Council, but are neither incorporated nor registered as autonomous charities. In addition, there are two "Associated Schools", which are independent schools in the course of achieving full status . . . Also there are a number of "Affiliated Schools" . . . which pay a small subscription and take part in some joint activities. The charity takes no part in the financing or administration of these schools. All orders, contracts of service (etc) are made in the name of the regional companies . . . All other assets and liabilities of the charity (including the not very extensive endowments) are held in the names of these regional companies . . . '

Membership

As might be supposed, the issue of who is or might reasonably be a member, and the rights and duties of that membership, is equally complicated:

'The trust has no "membership" as such, but the entire population of the area it serves could be said to have a rather similar status.'

'The charity has no register of members, although there are lists of their own memberships, maintained by the various sections. In fact, every resident in the area is *ipso facto* a member of the charity . . .'

'There are about 62,000 voting members, with a further class of non-voting associates . . . Voting members are members of the company-limited-by-guarantee . . .' [The quotation from this charity with respect to its number of branches etc explains the existence of the 'non-voting associates'.]

'. . . tenant/resident representatives participate in the work of two of the subcommittees. There is also a system of Area Management Committees, with more local concerns.'

'. . . there are about 50,000 individuals and organisations holding "clients"' discretionary accounts with the charity. The donors can require their balances to be distributed to organisations which are charitable in UK law . . . so these accounts form a series of "bubble trusts" within the charity. To that extent, subscribers to the charity have some powers over its operations.'

'What this charity calls its "associate members" are actually its "volunteers". Because it is a company-limited-by-guarantee, it must also have members who are registered as such . . . In fact, neither the directors nor the regular donors are so registered; it is thought that the only registered guarantors are the two subscribers to the original application to form the company.'

'The charity has about 30,000 members, who . . . pay a regular subscription of £33 . . . The charity has some very substantial capital donors, and these can become [members] if they specifically request it. In addition there are also over 200,000 ordinary members who have no voting rights (i.e. they are regular subscribers below the financial level required of [full members]).'

'The trustees are both the directors and the members of the company-limited-by-guarantee.' [NB This very large charity has some 800 fundraising branches, with 17,000 members who have to content themselves with the 'national public meeting'.]

'The charity has no members, in the sense of a group entitled to attend some form of AGM . . . However, there are a number of "friends" who might be seen to have some sort of status within the charity.'

'The charity's [trustees] are its members, and these control both the regional companies . . . and the Corporation as a whole . . . Also, there are [non-trustee] governors of the individual schools, who have some status within their own schools . . . The "associated" and "affiliated" schools . . . are not seen as having any sort of "membership" . . .'

All the charities with some type of membership have some sort of AGM (in addition to a principal meeting of its trustees), if only that required by company law. There are a few peculiarities:

'The Trust is required to hold an area meeting for the general public.'

'There is an AGM for the volunteer/associate members; it has no powers . . . There is no formal meeting of the members of the company, nor does it appear that any elective resolutions have been passed, dispensing with holding such meetings, or laying accounts before them . . .'

'. . . branches also send delegates to a national public meeting . . . this charity possesses an extremely active President, who concerns herself with both fundraising and relief operations; however, she takes no part in the administration . . .'

Charity 18 does hold AGMs for the 'members' of the companies-limited-by-shares that form its regional companies.

'. . . the Corporate Executive . . . consist[s] of the President, five chairs of the regional companies, plus five [trustees]. Each trustee holds one of the 100 shares in each of the limited regional companies; the remaining shares are held by the charity itself.'

Volunteers and staff

Although we commonly talk about 'the voluntary sector', the status of a volunteer is not always clear:

'There are no "volunteers" actually engaged by the Trust itself; a number operate within the hospital, but they are attached to the League of Friends, the Red Cross, the WRVS and so on.'

'The very wide spectrum of the charity's activities is almost entirely carried out by a large number of appointed volunteers, drawn from the membership, who both provide expertise and carry out executive functions. In addition . . . members are expected to do some fundraising as well . . .'

'The charity has no voluntary workers as such, but tenants and others may undertake small-scale fundraising activities for their local purposes.'

'However, about six "experts" are currently working on various in-house projects, who have been seconded to the charity by their employers.'

'The 20,000 members may all be considered to be volunteers, engaged on a wide variety of duties.'

'The charity has about 17,000 voluntary workers, who are the members of its fundraising branches. It has no voluntary workers overseas, where it is a matter of policy to *employ* local people on a temporary basis.'

Charity employment practices have few differences from those of other employers; however, there are one or two points about some of the senior paid officials:

'The senior paid staff [were] originally appointed by the local authority, although one is now a staff appointment at the school itself . . .'

'The Act setting up the charity makes specific reference only to a Director "whom the trustees may choose to appoint" and "a secretary and such other officers and servants" as may be appropriate. The Act is silent as to what their specific duties may be, which may have the effect of inhibiting the delegation of authority within the charity.'

It seemed fair to ask the rather pointed question 'Have there been any thefts?', as embezzlement by charity staff has been reported. The meagre number reported here seem to have occurred in large charities with numerous branches. Although one of the larger and more recent frauds happened in a subsidiary, rather than a branch, it is obvious that branches are very open to (small-scale) fraud. Most of the 'local fundraising efforts' are for cash, as are flag days and house-to-house collections; all these charities have regulations designed to prevent fraud in these areas, but few of those we have spoken to seem to be under any illusions about the degree of compliance that can be enforced against voluntary workers. A few quotations may give a good idea of what occurs:

'There has been one major case of embezzlement in recent years, which was detected after a very few months. It resulted in no loss to the charity, because the bank refunded the monies that had gone astray.'

'There was one case of embezzlement about fifteen years ago. No prosecution resulted.'

'There have been no instances of embezzlement as such, but there has been a moderately large loss of funds from an overseas bank, which is probably the result of fraud by the bank's officers.'

The proper control of both the methods of operations and the proportionate costs of fundraisers is rightly seen as a major aspect of any system of financial governance within a charity. In fact, only a minority in our sample of charities actually made much use of *designated* fundraisers, either as employees or as consultants. A few more quotations may give the picture:

'The League of Friends undertakes a good deal of work of this sort . . . Although these initiatives are independent of the Trust, the Chairman plays a substantial role in their activities. It is thought that his considerable experience of health service administration will ensure that any direct solicitations from the public will be conducted in a proper manner.'

'The charity seldom undertakes fundraising at national level . . . However, a good deal is undertaken locally: instructions on Charity Act requirements have been distributed.'

'. . . this charity has a peculiar problem over fundraising. Its founder dispersed his considerable fortune to his family and a number of family trusts, leaving a comparatively modest endowment for this [charity]. However, its name, together with the presence of family members among the trustees, makes it virtually impossible to attract substantial sums . . . '

'The charity does not regularly employ professional fundraisers, although members of staff do solicit specific assistance and donations from time to time . . . The charity does not give permission to use the charity's name or logo. However, the charity has made use of the names and logos of sponsors in certain cases.'

'. . . the volunteer/associate members all do some fundraising, and the Administrator is of the opinion that about 80% of her time is devoted to this. None of these people has any qualification or special expertise in fundraising – nor do they know anything at all about any Codes of Practice in the area . . . Direct mail shots have been used to raise funds, but no specific instructions have been formulated about this.'

'It is believed that both the professional and the in-house fundraisers conform with the codes of practice issued by the Institute of Charity Fundraising Managers . . . The charity allows its name to be used by external organisations for reward, in a number of joint ventures in which its name etc appears with those of the other party. Such ventures are always the subject of written agreements and conform to a policy established by the Fundraising Committee.'

'Senior members of staff do apply for grants and attempt to raise funds for specific and usually substantial items, from time to time.'

Summary and issues

Our sample includes charities with no members other than their trustees, others that give the title of 'member' to substantial regular subscribers, and at least one in which the volunteers are treated in much the same way. At least one of our sample will give life membership to a donor of a substantial capital sum. A possible definition of a member (other than a trustee) might be a person with a right to receive copies of the annual report and to attend at an annual general meeting. This is obviously the case with companies-limited-by-guarantee, although we have seen one case where there are considerable numbers of volunteers and regular subscribers but it is only the trustees who have membership of the company!

Several respondent charities have 'presidents', who commonly preside at the AGMs. Their role is otherwise often uncertain and may be largely inactive. As has been said, where this is not the case, they usually appear in the roles of high-profile volunteers.

Although we have discussed the possible functions of a president in a charity's administrative structure, we did not even raise the issue of 'patrons' with our respondents. The larger charities certainly have them (who are often members of the Royal Family) but we felt that, whilst such patrons play an important part, it is not in the administration of a charity. This does, however, raise a question of what is meant by 'governance': *prima facie*, it relates to the administrative system but the background to the setting up of the Cadbury Committee, for example, suggests a concern about public confidence in an administration rather than its mere existence. Charities and other organisations appear to seek patronage to advance their credibility. To the extent that this credibility relates to the charity's stability and the probity of its administration, patronage could be seen as a form of accreditation and hence of governance itself.

The functions of an AGM commonly include the right to nominate and appoint directors/trustees and other officers, to reappoint the auditors and to 'accept' the accounts. In a general way, it would seem appropriate in a modern charity for these rights to be available to the widest class of those who make meaningful contributions toward the support of the charity.

POINTS FOR DISCUSSION

3a Whether all members should have the right to receive copies of the annual report and accounts, attend an AGM and vote thereat.

3b Whether the AGM should have powers to elect non-executive trustees and other officers; to reappoint the auditors and to receive the annual report and accounts.

3c Whether the Chair at such AGMs should be taken by an appointed or elected president, who is not a trustee.

A closely related issue for national and international charities is the status of their branches. These can be autonomous or non-autonomous in a legal sense, depending on whether or not they are registered as separate charities with the Charity Commission. Nevertheless, our sample suggests that unregistered branches can have very many degrees of freedom. Some charities have a clearly federal style of organisation – perhaps to the extent that their 'branch committees' may take on virtually the whole of the *local* 'control, responsibility and management of the administration of the charity'. There was one case where such local organisations were quite clearly the centre of gravity of the charity, and where its regional and national apparatus were very slight.

Even in outwardly monolithic charities, very wide differences of approach were observed. One seemed to take fairly extreme measures to ensure the subordinate status of its branches, while another seemed to accept that, apart from their subscription payments, its branches tended to have their own agenda. Again, some branches are concerned only with fundraising (including the collection of membership subscriptions), while others combine fundraising with volunteer work on the charity's objects. One of our sample had two classes of branches – one for fundraising alone and the other devoted almost exclusively to volunteer work.

Large charities commonly interpose a regional structure between their branches and head office. In such cases there are often paid regional officers whose function is to expand, service and supervise the activities of the branches in their areas. There was some suggestion that these posts could be a source of friction, both with the branches etc and with head office. Officials might seem to be over-extending their initiative in the control they seek to exercise over 'their' branches; again, they might seem to be facilitating branch officers in the pursuit of branch agenda as against some national policy. We find it curious that, in at least two of our respondent charities, the full detail of the membership of those branches was recorded at regional level, with a less informative database maintained at head office.

The regions often play a part in the representation of the branches at national level, through the appointment of a regional chair, and perhaps other officers at that level. The 'federal' respondent had an interesting variant, in that the assets and contracts of its branches were held at regional level; it may be that in that case the regional trustees were acting as custodian trustees for the constituent branches.

POINTS FOR **DISCUSSION**

3d Whether charities should draw up the regulations relating to branches so as to make it clear to what extent, if at all, branches or regions can act in an autonomous fashion.

3e Whether the remits of regional paid officials should be drawn up in a precise manner, so as to determine their responsibilities and authorities both with respect to the branches etc and to the charity as a whole.

CHAPTER FOUR

Numbers of trustees

Table 2 sets out some basic data about the numbers of trustees and their status, but the complexity of most charities' arrangements in this matter means that considerable care must be exercised in interpreting it.

Role of trustees

Where two figures appear in the 'Number of trustees' column, the second figure relates to non-voting members, who are usually the 'Hon. trustees', as can be seen from column 8: these are people whom the charity has wanted to honour in some way, and they have no duties or (one supposes) responsibilities toward the charity. In Charity 15, such appointments amount to nearly one-half of the number of the active trustees. However, in Charity 10, the split was explained like this:

'There are seven Managing Trustees and three Ordinary Trustees. The latter used to control the assets, in the days when the Foundation had close connections with the founder's company, but this is no longer the case . . . Nowadays, long-serving Managing Trustees are, so to speak, "kicked upstairs", but the office is not completely ceremonial, as will be seen.' [An Ordinary Trustee still serves on the charity's Investment Policy Committee – and these trustees approve the payment of a fee to the Managing Trustees.]

In Charity 4, the ten nominated members have no vote but are present in an advisory capacity; in Charity 8, this is the case with the 36 regional representatives. A couple of the other respondents have two ranks of trustee but the distinction is entirely honorific.

Seven of these charities have between ten and fifteen trustees, and one might suppose that this represents the upper limit to the size of a group which can truly be said to take executive decisions. However, it can be seen that, if one considers only the 'Elected/appointed' column, a further seven charities fall within these limits. In these cases, one might wonder about the exact functions (and levels of activity) of the other classes of trustee.

Charities 1 and 17 are respectively an NHS trust and a university; the five *ex officio* trustees of the former are its full-time executive directors, the two at the university are its Vice Chancellor and the President of its Students' Union. The *ex officio* trustees in the other three cases seem largely honorary appointments of people such as Lord Mayors and Lords Lieutenant.

Six of our eighteen charities have 'Nominated representatives', trustees who are appointed by outside bodies. At Charity 9 the 26

TABLE 2 NUMBERS OF TRUSTEES AND THEIR STATUS

Charity	Number of trustees	Elected and/or appointed	Ex officio	Nominated representatives	Regional representatives	Co-opted	Honorary trustees	Term of office (years)	Longest serving trustee (years)
1	11	6	5	0	0	0	0	2/4	1
2	15	13	0	2	0	0	0	3	6
3	48	26	0	0	22	0	0	No limit	25
4	44+10	9	0	10	30	5	0	3	10+
5	12	9	0	3	0	0	0	Life	20+
6	12+1	9	0	3	0	0	1	3	9
7	13	13	0	0	0	0	0	3	17
8	14+36	14	0	0	36	0	0	3	28
9	52	26	0	26	0	0	0	3	15–20
10	7+3	10	0	0	0	0	0	5	10+
11	10	10	0	0	0	0	0	Life	8
12	74+20	66	8	0	0	0	20	1	30
13	28	15	0	0	10	3	0	3	20+
14	17	8	0	0	9	0	0	3	6
15	23+12	5	9	9	0	0	12	3	20+
16	30	8	6	0	16	0	0	3	10
17	20	13+2	2	0	0	3	0	3	10+
18	150+20	150	0	0	0	0	20	To 70	30+

such appointments equal the number of the elected/appointed trustees, whilst at Charity 15 they exceed them by nine to five. One cannot emphasise too often that great care must be taken before coming to any conclusion based on any of these numerical 'facts' about charity trustees. In the case of Charity 9 it has been observed:

'This arrangement can produce occasional conflicts of aims: sometimes Council members can consider themselves as representatives of particular outside interests, rather than trustees of the charity in its entirety.'

Charity 2 also reported that its nominated trustees rarely attend, except to make representations on behalf of the body that appoints them. On the other hand, the elected trustee who was interviewed from Charity 15 had formed the opinion that these nominated representatives play an informed and valuable role in its affairs.

Six of the respondent charities have specifically designated 'Regional representatives', forming a significant proportion of the total number of trustees. These charities all have a number of branches, and their representatives are commonly the branch chairs. Several report occasional conflicts of interest arising from these appointments. However, Charity 16 makes a special point of ensuring that such people act in a truly dual capacity: they transmit the views of their branches before the executive decisions are taken but thereafter convey those decisions as policy to their branches.

Moreover, most of the other charities with branches receive many, if not the majority, of their nominations for election from their branches. Especially where charities with branches also have very large numbers of trustees, one must wonder whether they may be acting as elected representatives of the branch organisations. Charity 16 is firmly organised on those lines.

Summary and issues

One might wonder whether there is some optimal size for a Board of Trustees. The sample shows a wide variation in the numbers of trustees, ranging from ten to 170, and since these charities are all viable, it would seem probable that there is more than one criterion for size of the board to be considered. It is well known that a group which is required to take *action* is likely to be more effective if its membership lies in the range of three to twelve because these numbers are the limits of what a chair can hope to control as a decision-making unit; a greater number is likely to become a debating chamber.

But that brings us to an important point. Action is what is required of *executive management*, where something must be done to fulfil some policy decision imposed from above. Here *consensus* between a small, like-minded group is likely to be the most effective way of deciding what must be done, and doing it. But this is not so obvious with respect to policy-making itself. A very wide range of possible courses of action may be available to achieve quite simple ends; the alternatives are not always compatible, so compromises are not always possible or even desirable. The issues do need to be *debated*, and even put to a vote.

In the latter case, the most effective debate will be one at which the greatest variety of possible courses of action will be canvassed. The board should contain representatives from the whole range of regional and sectional interests, and it is obvious that this is the rationale behind the very large bodies of trustees that we have encountered. The existence of the smaller bodies may indicate that a more limited range of possibilities needs to be represented in the policy-making process in those charities.

Another important issue with respect to trustees is the term of office for which they are appointed, to which must be added the limits placed on reappointment – and the length of time that people actually serve. Two of the charities reappoint their trustees annually, and a further three appoint them for life (in one case with an upper age limit of 70). The others appoint for between three and five years, the majority going for three-year terms. Two charities report limits on the number of times a person can stand for election, two others 'actively discourage' more than two/three re-elections, another requires a fallow year after a number of terms. Three also vary these rules slightly for officers. The maximum terms reported are 30 years or more, but in fact the average service of those currently elected seems to be three to six years.

POINTS FOR **DISCUSSION**

4a Whether a charity should establish a council whose primary purpose is the setting of policy.

4b Whether this council should be large enough to provide representation for all the regional and sectional interests that have relevance to its objects.

4c Whether the membership of other, purely executive, committees should number between three and twelve.

4d Whether trustees should continue to serve beyond the age of 70, or for longer than (say) six years without a break.

CHAPTER FIVE

Trustees: their nomination and selection

There are a number of stereotypes that many people outside the voluntary sector commonly apply to charity trustees – 'the Great and the Good' among them. It is interesting to see how some of our respondents prefer to categorise them:

'The "background" of the non-executive directors commonly includes service with some Health Authority, either as a manager or as a board member. Otherwise the Chairman is a retired army officer, and the other members include a local councillor, business people and a retired doctor.'

'. . . the long-serving nature of the Committee has produced one major problem; they are all white Anglo-Saxons in an area where the inhabitants are now 50% Asian and 10% Afro-Caribbean. That said, the efforts of the paid officers to persuade ethnic candidates to stand for office have not so far proved successful.'

'. . . 40% sufferers from the medical condition which the charity was formed to assist; 20% "carers" for sufferers; 20 consultants or other health professionals specialising in that complaint; 15% others.'

'. . . it should be borne in mind that the Housing Corporation's monitoring procedures require the *curriculum vitae* of each of the trustees to be submitted to the Corporation. In fact, the social position and traditions of the "family" trustees ensure a fairly high-powered body of trustees, which has few problems over complying with the required criteria of membership.'

'. . . about half . . . have extensive experience in banking, finance and investment; the remainder include those with experience in the civil service, local government, law, trade unionism and academia.'

'The background of the elected trustees is very varied indeed, and reflects the wide public interest in the activities of this charity; the largest discernible group are university teachers! Given the prominence of the charity, it may not be unfair to make reference to "the Great and the Good", although such people are much less in evidence among the elected members of Council than among those who are appointed from elsewhere.'

'Three doctors; one SRN [this is a medical charity]; one solicitor; one ex-service officer; two people with their own businesses; two unknown . . .'

'. . . pretty well divided between the (professionally relevant) "Great and the Good", professionals such as accountants, lawyers and . . . engineers, people running their own businesses and (our own) "volunteers".'

'. . . two veterinary surgeons, a solicitor, two people with their own businesses, three academics and two other teachers – the remainder appear to be largely retired people.'

'The "list of requirements" includes finance and banking experience, business management, medical accounting and legal qualification, and experience overseas; however, most members "qualify" under several heads.'

'. . . the common factor of most elected members is active branch membership.'

Professional background

In other respects they may be uncomfortably close to a fair sample of the senior trustees of British charities: there were no members of minority groups among them and only one woman, who was also the founder of her charity. Their professional backgrounds are as follows (in many cases the description is of what they did before their retirement or semi-retirement):

4 merchant bankers and bank managers

3 'professional people' in practice or consultancy

2 senior academics

1 state registered nurse

3 civil servants or local government officers

1 teacher (who was also a trades union secretary)

2 company directors

Could these people be described as 'the Great and the Good'? Four or five of them certainly do hold, or have held, senior positions in substantial organisations, but we doubt whether their names or faces are known to the readers of *Hello* magazine or the *Tatler*.

Trustees and their charities

Turning to the role of trustees seen from the perspective of the sixteen trustees we interviewed, Table 3 summarises their responses concerning other trusteeships, directorships, public office and so on.

TABLE 3 TRUSTEES AND THEIR CHARITIES

Trustee	Other trusteeships?	(Other) company directorships?	Any public offices?	Member of Rotary, TA etc?	Knows other trustees?	Meets paid officials of charity?
A	0	0	Deputy Lieutenant	No	No	1 × 2 weeks
B	2	0	Professional body	No	No	Frequently
C	3	0	Professional body	No	Professionally	Several × weekly
D	2	2	No	No	2 friends	Rarely
E	2	1	No	No	Club members	1 × 2 weeks
F	1	5	No	Livery Company	Rarely	Frequently
G	0	0	No	No	1 friend	2 × week
H	2	2	No	Political party	Rarely	2 × week
I	0	0	No	Trade union secretary	Rarely	Most days
J	0	1	No	No	1 business acquaintance	500 hours per year
K	3	5	Deputy Lieutenant	No	Club members	2 × month
L	1	0	No	No	No	Frequently
M	1	0	No	No	No	2 × week
N	2	4	No	Political party	No	Frequently
O	1	1	Parish councillor	No	1 slightly	2 × week
P	0	0	No	No	No	Around meetings

There were no trustees who figured on the boards of a great many charities; Trustees C and K achieve their numbers only by (properly) including a college fellowship and a lay trusteeship at a cathedral. The company directorships were commonly non-executive appointments, often enough in family businesses. It was interesting to see how few reported public office or membership of things such as Rotary, the Territorial Army (TA) and so on; no doubt the frequency of their meetings with the paid officials of their charity (and the board/committee meetings themselves) represented a sufficient commitment of time for most people. Moreover, the large number of former local or central government officers commonly observed that their jobs had actually prohibited seeking public office.

The last two columns of Table 3 are more significant. Given the oligarchic fashion in which almost all the sample charities *de facto* find their new trustees, it is inevitable that most of them will know one or two fellow trustees – one has, somehow, to be 'known about'. The references to club membership probably need clarification: both refer to sports clubs whose activities impinge on those of a charity. Too much need not be read into these 'acquaintances'. Many of the sample of charities have their concerns in some fairly narrow area of interest, where most people who share that interest must be expected to know most of the others. These are rarely 'particular friendships'; one of the paid officials used the phrase 'cordial but not cosy' to describe the atmosphere at a typical meeting.

Indeed, one might be more interested in the six who do not claim some outside acquaintances on their boards. One was *ex officio* and another was, so to speak, head-hunted as possessing some desired criteria; the remainder had become 'known' to the charity through fairly lengthy connections with its work, in one capacity or another.

The amount of time required of office-holders is apparent from the last column. Trustee J is the non-executive director of the NHS trust, who is of course, paid for the work. His views were these:

'NHS trusts have a commitment to "openness", which is reflected in the phenomenal number of subcommittees they set up. Their purpose is to ensure that any substantial executive decision is passed before at least one non-executive director. The result is that non-executive directors find themselves compelled to plough through enormous quantities of paperwork. One might wonder whether this detailed appraisal of *executive* decisions is consistent with a non-executive (policy-making) status. It seems to be almost an additional function, akin to an inspectorate . . .'

(It might be noted that several of our respondent trustees other than Trustee J listed Area Health Authority memberships among their current or former activities. One might wonder whether the NHS may not provide experience of some very 'heavy duty' trusteeship indeed, which well equips any survivors for further work in any part of the voluntary sector.)

Selection of trustees

The methods of selecting the trustees range from the totally democratic to the unashamedly dynastic! The vast majority of our sample charities are effectively oligarchic, although many are theoretically more democratic in nature: this probably reflects the difficulty of finding people willing to undertake the responsibility and time-consuming labour of the task – except in a few high-profile or actually remunerated instances. This is an issue to which we will to let most of the respondents speak for themselves.

'[T]he first chairman was nominated by the Regional Health Authority, and, after consultation with the General Manager, the Medical Superintendent and the Director of Operations, the name was forwarded to the Secretary of State for approval. The remaining non-executive directors emerged from a list prepared by the Chairman, and forwarded to the Secretary of State for approval. Since that time, there have been considerable expressions of public concern at the way in which such appointments were made at certain other NHS healthcare trusts. It seems certain that future nominations will emerge from more open procedures, involving the advertisement of vacancies and consultations with local authorities.'

'Nominations have to be posted up for one month before the AGM. In fact, the full-time officers find extreme difficulty in persuading any "new blood" to stand for office . . . The "elections" take place at the AGM, at which no more than 20–25 people are present.'

'Twenty-two trustees are elected by the charity's 22 geographical regions; the remaining 26 are elected by the whole membership by postal ballot, one-third in each year.'

'Six trustees are elected to office by a direct vote of the membership, and a further three are elected by a regional vote; 31 trustees are the elected senior trustees, chairmen of committees or regional bodies.'

'The Trust deed requires that nine of the trustees be descendants of the founder [X], or his brother's [Y] male descendants. Of the remainder, one each is appointed by [one of the local universities], the City of [Z] and [a religious organisation]. It follows that any consultations over these appointments occur within the [X] family and the three institutions. It will happen that, when vacancies occur, the Trust may have some view as to who might make a suitable candidate, and this is communicated to the sponsors – sometimes, but not always, with success.'

'The trustees appointed by the charity itself are nominated after discussion by the Chairman and the Executive Director, and appointed by the Board of Trustees . . . Only nine of the trustees are appointed in this way; the remaining three are nominees of [another charitable body], including *ex officio* that body's Chairman.'

'Candidates for election can be nominated by any ten members of the charity. It should be noted that this charity is one that excites considerable enthusiasm among its membership – and the public at large! From time to time, concerted efforts are made by single-interest groups to influence its policy, as they have every right to do. The Council takes very real notice of what is said at the AGM, so this supplies a good idea of the views of the more active membership; however, it is very rarely that such movements can muster sufficient support to nominate *and* elect a Member of Council. Elected Members of Council are elected . . . by a ballot of the membership at the AGM. Members can nominate proxies to vote for particular candidates, if they think fit. A considerable number of "open" proxies are given to the Chairman.'

'Trustees are nominated for office by members . . . All trustees are elected to office at the national AGM, with the President and Treasurer elected separately, nine members elected for England (twice each year) and a further trustee each for Scotland and Wales. (Regional safeguards in England ensure a geographical spread.)'

'Candidates for Managing Trustee emerge from consultations between the existing trustees and the senior officers of the Foundation . . . Their appointment is confirmed by a meeting of the trustees . . .'

'Candidates for election can be nominated by any member . . . of the charity, but in practice this right is never exercised. *De facto*, a list of suggested replacements for vacancies is arrived at by the Chairman and his deputies and the Director, following some criteria for what is considered to be a well-balanced Committee of Management. Names are often also submitted by existing trustees . . . All elected members are re-elected annually . . . at the AGM . . . There is no postal ballot and no proxies; trustees are elected by the 500 or so [members] present and voting.'

'[C]andidates are put forward for election by existing Council Members, after consultation among trustees, directors and members of the advisory committees . . . Candidates are voted into office by the Council.'

'Vacancies among the local trustees are filled from nominees suggested by the Executive Committee . . . The local trustees are elected to office . . . at the Annual Meeting of the Trustees and Guardians. Representative trustees . . . serve for three years, when a further nomination is sought from the body in question.'

'[T]rustees who are not *ex officio* (or nominated from branches) are nominated by the Chairman after consultation with fellow trustees and senior officers . . . and are re-elected by the members voting in person at the AGM.'

'Lay governor members of the Board are recommended for office . . . by an Appointments Committee, which works from a "wanted" list of desired qualifications.'

'Candidates for [trusteeship] are nominated and elected by the regional companies, often from among the [non-trustee] governors of schools in their region . . . All must be communicant members of the Church of England.'

Induction of new trustees

Newly elected members in all but two of these charities receive a 'package' of documents, often including publications on the duties and responsibilities of charity trustees from the Charity Commission or the NCVO. Two (including one of those that do not give out documents) are mounting courses to improve the understanding of existing trustees. Nine invite such people to the head office, to meet the chief executive, see something of the organisation and take part in some additional orientation activities. These meetings often attempt to discover the particular interests and capacities of the new trustee.

Many of the respondents point to the fact that their newly appointed people commonly have considerable experience either as voluntary workers in the organisation or as trustees/directors of other organisations. One charity requires *candidates for election* to sign a formal acceptance of duties and responsibilities if elected. Another is equally forthright:

'Candidates for office are sent a list of the duties of a trustee. If elected, they attend a briefing at Central Office, and also receive a "pack" of literature on trusteeship issued by the Charity Commission and others. Finally they are voted into office by the Council, and required to sign the minute book as evidence that they understand what is expected of them.'

In some charities, the right to nominate trustees is available to members but never exercised; in others, nominations emerge from discussions among senior existing trustees, sometimes with the aid of guidelines, or even subcommittees, aimed at securing an appropriate 'balance' on the Council.

Again, sometimes a complete list of nominees is voted in by a very small number of attendees at the AGM. Other charities provide postal ballots of all members; still others permit the use of proxies, where an overwhelming number of proxies are commonly given to the Chair – to be used as he or she thinks fit. These problems seem inevitable in a nation-wide organisation, where only the very keen and the more well-to-do retired are likely to make time to travel to some central AGM. This may be avoided to some extent if the charity has a branch organisation; elections may be organised though the branches, or branch or regional chairs may become 'senatorial' trustees. However, some charities have members who are not attached to branches, and so hold both 'branch' and 'national' elections.

Summary and issues

The election of trustees is another area where charities seem to fall into one or other of two disparate groups. In many charities there is no great desire on anybody's part to become a trustee, and filling vacancies on Council is usually a matter of exerting pressure on people to stand. This may be unsurprising, given the amount of time and the responsibilities usually involved. One might also surmise that, in those charities, concerned people have little difficulty in making their views on their charity's administration known to those in office – and that those views are usually complied with. However, in others the situation is very different, and people feel very strongly and contentiously about a whole range of issues, and about the degree to which advocates of those issues find representation on the Council and Board of the charity.

Such charities may become the target of a variety of 'single issue' pressure groups. Those groups are not necessarily undesirable; in any case, one person's pressure group is another person's 'big issue'. In fact, many of our respondents clearly make positive use of such movements – by identifying them and inviting them to nominate representatives or even trustees. This also has the benefit of confining their influence to agreed limits. What is undesirable is attempts by such groups to hijack other, larger, multi-issue organisations by clandestine means.

Officials, paid and unpaid, and especially branch officers, need to be aware of the danger of attempted take-overs by extreme interests – and need to convey those concerns to their trustees and members *in advance of the assault*. Counter-measures are at hand: presumably the reason that the group has not been invited to nominate representatives is that its objects are seen to be too extreme, so the charity's regulations should include clauses authorising the expulsion of members who advocate them. Again, the regulations could forbid the organisation of 'a party within the Party', to make clandestine activity more difficult.

More generally, membership secretaries need to be alert to possible 'padding' of their electoral rolls. Perhaps the qualifying subscriptions and voluntary service requirements need to be made fairly substantial, and be in place for several years, before voting rights are obtained. In times when single-issue politics seems to be overtaking the more traditional multi-issue type, it may be that submersion by extremists is a fitting penalty for failure to take suitable precautions against them.

POINTS FOR **DISCUSSION**

5a Whether charities should draft their regulations with respect to membership with especial care, so as to ensure that only *bona fide* supporters of their aims can be admitted, or retain membership.

5b Whether charities should grant 'membership status' to all such supporters who assist with their work in a regular and substantial fashion over a suitable period of time.

No doubt the less democratic methods of nominating and appointing trustees, described above, are seen as another defence against extremism. A more positive advantage of the oligarchic method of selecting trustees is said to be that mature decisions can be reached, securing the appointment of competent people possessing an appropriate range of skills. The benefit is not self-evident: apart from an admitted tendency to recruit more 'people like us', this method is better adapted to the selection of executive trustees. There, a consensus between the like-minded is helpful, but in the equally important matter of policy-making this consensus may prevent adequate exploration of the full range of possibilities open to the charity.

One might also question the counter-proposition that more democratic methods will produce people who are not only unsuited to executive activity but also too wild and unrepresentative in their views to be useful policy-makers. The same arguments might apply to elections for central and local government, but in fact the separation of tasks between the elected members and the executive seems to produce a system that works well enough in most cases.

Unfortunately, the big difference between government elections and those in charities is the presence of substantial multi-issue party political machines. These select 'their' candidates in the first instance, and they are usually at pains to secure people who might be fit to hold office and are sufficiently disciplined to adhere to a coherent 'party line'. Again, the machine 'gets out the vote' – and in doing so, is as likely to alert its opponents as to bring out its supporters. Finally, after the election, the party 'whips in' its representatives, and ensures that they *do* follow the 'correct' policies.

This machinery is unlikely to exist in the voluntary sector – except perhaps in something like an NHS healthcare trust, in which the universality of the need for its services *might* make it a suitable target for conventional party politics. In the absence of political machinery, the reaction of charity members to something they don't like tends to be that of company shareholders: they vote with their feet – and cancel their subscriptions or sell their shares. They do this despite the possible existence of substantial and hardly realised assets and potential, because they do not think it worth while getting involved as individuals in a fight with obviously well-organised interests.

Nevertheless, modern ideas of 'open governance' in an 'open society' favour the adoption of more democratic methods for the selection of charity trustees. The problem is that these methods are likely to produce trustees who may be better suited to policy-making than executive management. This in turn seems to favour an 'elected representative' model of governance, but that model is not well suited to many charities, which actually need executive trustees.

However, all charities need some non-executive trustees, and it might be argued that it is those trustees who need to be selected in a democratic fashion, because it is they who are charged with the representation of the public interest. Not even the most enthusiastic libertarians seem to advocate the appointment of employees by democratic vote – and it is probable that many executive trustees will be paid officials as well.

POINTS FOR DISCUSSION

5c Whether candidates for the office of non-executive trustee should be nominated by the membership.

5d Whether, if a charity has branches, votes for elections to national office should be made by those attending branch AGMs, wherever possible.

5e Whether, unless the membership is substantially local in nature, any charity-wide elections to national office should be by postal ballot.

5f Whether proxy-voting should be discouraged.

CHAPTER SIX

Nomenclature applied to trustees

Our sample reveals considerable diversity of titles given to trustees, both in absolute terms and in the qualifications attached to them. They are summarised in Table 4.

Summary and issues

There is evidence (although not in our sample!) that some people in such positions may not be aware that they *are* trustees. In any case, the nomenclature and surrounding circumstances of the appointment of some members of those bodies makes their status less certain.

It must be admitted that 'Trustee of All Souls' and 'the Chair of Trustees of Balliol' would not have quite the ring of their current equivalents; moreover, in the case of the collegiate universities, it would also underline the differing status of 'junior fellows', 'professorial fellows' and the like. In the same way, someone who currently bears a title such as 'Director General' might be less happy with 'Chief Executive Trustee', especially if that meant spelling out whether he (or she) or the senior non-executive trustee was actually 'the Chair of Trustees'.

But these distinctions are significant: it is important for those administering an existing charity to know who is and who is not a trustee. This is especially the case with Chief Executive Officers, and other senior executives, who may have no policy-making responsibilities at all, if these are reserved to trustees who have been 'elected' to that office. However, as has been said, it is obvious that the senior paid officials play a major role in the policy-making of several of our charities, and general observation suggests that this will be the case in many others. It follows that these paid officials must be trustees under the terms of the Charities Acts, and, further, that there are 'executive trustees', and therefore other 'non-executive trustees'.

TABLE 4 NOMENCLATURE OF TRUSTEES

Charity	Title of 'trustees'	Title of 'chair'	Title of 'chief executive'	Non-trustees on subcommittees?
1	Non-executive directors	Chair	Chief Executive	Yes
2	Trustees	Chair	Senior Community Officer	No
3	Trustees	Chairman	Chief Executive	No
4	Trustees	Chairman	Chief Executive and Company Secretary	Yes
5	Trustees	Chairman	Chief Executive	Yes
6	Trustees	Chairman	Chief Executive	No
7	Trustees	Chair	National Director	No
8	Trustees/ Directors	Chair	Chief Executive	Yes
9	Trustees	Chairman	Director General	Yes
10	Managing Trustees and Ordinary Trustees	Chairman	Director	Yes
11	Trustees	Chair	Administrator and Head of Care Services	No
12	Vice-presidents and Committee Members	Chairman	Director and Secretary	Yes
13	Trustees	Chairman	Director General	Yes
14	Trustees	Chair	Director General	Yes
15	Trustees and Guardians	Chairman	Director	No
16	Trustees	Chairman	Controller	Yes
17	Governors	Chairman	Chief Executive	Yes
18	Fellows	President	Registrar	Yes

POINT FOR DISCUSSION

6a Whether all trustees should include the word 'trustee' in their title.

Executive and non-executive trustees

The probability that the full-time paid senior executives may be truly members of the Board of Trustees makes the role of the non-executive trustees especially important. They have the duty of representing the interests of both the charity's membership (if any) and the public interest at large. It seems essential that these people should be specifically appointed to fulfil that role, and that there should be a sufficient number of them to make their influence felt. Given the 'public purposes' nature of a charity, it may be appropriate for them to be of an equal number-plus-one with the executive trustees, and for the Chair of the Board of Trustees to be chosen from among the non-executive members.

Our sample suggests that some unpaid trustees can have executive functions, and thus actually be executive trustees. Theoretically, there could be paid non-executive trustees, but we shall argue that the hallmark of a voluntary organisation is that its non-executive trustees are unpaid. There is a well-known dispensation for normal fees being payable to trustees who are professionally qualified, but our sample also includes two cases in which other non-executive trustees are being paid, and another where the issue is a matter of contention between the charity and the Charity Commissioners. It would seem that these payments relate neither to executive nor to strictly non-executive activity, but to situations in which the trustees are called on to act as 'inspectors' for the proper handling of certain highly sensitive issues by the charity. The Charity Commission's view of such payments seemed to be influenced by the presence or absence of some external or at least uninvolved person(s) to verify the justification of the amounts so paid.

POINTS FOR DISCUSSION

6b Whether the existence of classes of executive trustees and non-executive trustees should be recognised.

6c Whether the number of non-executive trustees should be at least equal to that of the executive trustees, plus one, and their Chair should be drawn from among them.

6d Whether it should be recognised that executive trustees can be employees of their charities, and remunerated accordingly, but that no payments should normally be made to non-executive trustees (except for out-of-pocket expenses).

6e Whether appropriate fees may be paid to non-executive trustees who act for the charity in a professional capacity, which may include the

The general policy of the Charity Commission is to give (grudging?) approval to the appointment of one paid trustee, and this would appear to be seen as 'best practice' in the USA as well. We would argue that, while we appreciate the view that charity trustees ought not 'to be in it for the money', the ruling just does not accord with practice. Chief Executives of 'not-for-profit businesses' – and their teams of senior managers – very obviously act as their profit-making counterparts, in the roles of managing director, finance director, sales director and so on. It is not possible to divide the policy-making from the executive management of a commercial enterprise: the trading provides the money, and the money dictates the range of feasible policy alternatives.

The title 'trustee'

It is equally important that the title of trustee not be given to those who do not have 'the general control, responsibility and management of the administration of [the] charity'. Table 2 gives several instances in which this might be a matter for debate. A typical but difficult example is the 'honorary trustee', who clearly has no such status. Given the general acceptance and understanding of such things as 'honorary doctorates', that particular term might be spared: it is hard to conceive of a better one that precisely captures its reality. What is less satisfactory is the common title 'life trustee'; honorary trustees do hold their titles for life, but our sample has two examples where *real* trustees are also appointed to office for life.

POINT FOR **DISCUSSION**

6g Whether the word 'trustee' should not be used in the title of any person who is not a trustee within the meaning of the Charities Act. The sole exception would be the use of the title 'honorary trustee' in cases where the person so named has no part whatsoever in the administration of the charity; in this regard, we suggest that the title 'life trustee' may be particularly misleading.

'*Ex officio* trustee' is a similarly confusing title. Our sample shows, for example, the Vice Chancellor and President of the Students' Union of a university in this category: they are often among the more active members of the Court of Governors. By contrast, other *ex officios* tend to be dignitaries, like the Lord Mayor of London, the Archbishop of Canterbury, the Chairman of the Baltic Exchange and so on, who no doubt wish the charities well but are rarely active attendees at meetings of trustees. Of itself, the title is nothing more nor less than evidence of another non-democratic method of appointing trustees, and there are certainly charities in which the Lord Mayor and the Archbishop will be entirely active, normal trustees. What is necessary is that the charities, and their *ex officios*, should be aware of what is expected of such appointees. If they are active, they are trustees; if not, perhaps they should be called something else.

'Co-opted trustees' sometimes have the same problem; usually they are appointed to be active, but at other times their activity is at least *de facto* quite limited. Typical cases are where Members of Parliament have this status, which seems to involve (unpaid!) representation of the charities' interests at Westminster rather than active exercise of control, responsibility etc. Again, the solution is to be sure what is expected of these people, and title them accordingly.

'Nominated representative trustees', who are sponsored by outside bodies, are a more complex problem. If the appointment is 'for real', one would need to consider whether the two charities should be considered to be 'related charities'. In one of our respondent charities, three of twelve trustees, including the Chairman, were nominated by one other charity, so some relationship might seem to exist between them. In another, no fewer than 26 such nominees from 26 separate organisations appear to face 26 elected trustees; the sheer number of sponsors suggests that some other interpretation of their role is required.

As with *ex officios*, the role of nominated representative trustee is not self-evident. The nominees and their sponsors may sincerely intend to take part in the administration of the host charity. On the other hand, it is clear that many do not, and their actions (or lack thereof) demonstrate the fact. This is another matter where a charity needs to *ask* the nominees and their sponsors what they propose as their contribution to the arrangement. We argue that the possibility of asking other bodies to nominate trustees or representatives is an important part of any charity's defences against more hostile interference.

There is a further complication: might not some *elected* trustees not merely fail to administer their charities in any way but actually be elected with an expectation that they will not administer them? Several of our respondents have substantial numbers of elected members; in some cases they are all found employment in various subcommittees, whether as chairs or as ordinary members. In others, they have no obvious *administrative* duties to perform beyond attendance at Council; we suggest that bare attendance at policy-making meetings may not give sufficient understanding of the executive actions of their charities to allow such people to function as non-executive trustees.

There is at least one high-level activity to be performed within a charity, which is not directly related to either policy-making or executive decision-taking. In one respondent charity, a spokesperson had no hesitation over describing the basic role of its trustees as 'ambassadorial', and the second (a trustee) likened the role to that of 'a constitutional monarch'. As such their job is to represent the charity to its members, other organisations and the community at large, and represent it in such a way as to reassure their audiences of the importance the charity is placing on the occasion. Presumably the nominated trustees in such a charity have the additional responsibility of representing their sponsors to the charity – at a similar level.

This ambassadorial function is quite consistent with the office of a trustee of the charity; one might hope that all trustees contribute to its activity in this way. On the other hand, the possibility of appointments being made *without either party supposing that the appointee assumed the full duties and responsibilities of a trustee* would account for the presence in our sample of so many people who clearly do not and cannot perform as trustees. In a few instances, such people may be called upon to assume administrative responsibilities in the charity by being appointed to serve on executive committees.

Such arrangements are hardly illogical. One might wonder whether the position of these 'bare' trustees in many charities might not be very like that of the 'supervisory board' in the two-tier boards to be found in continental European companies. In fact, our respondents disagreed with such an analogy, and their arguments are substantial: neither ambassadors nor constitutional monarchs can be said to supervise anything at all! In addition, these people are expected to convey an impression of greater weight than could be implied by a title that was clearly subsidiary to that of 'trustee'. Even more to the point, one of these respondent trustees pays tribute to the contribution of such people to Council meetings, where they often raise issues of importance; he says 'The Executive Committee can never take these people for granted'.

But what are they to be called? If they do not act as trustees, it is not appropriate that they make use of that word in their title. However, there are three distinct chains of command to be found in many charities. Besides the Chair and trustees, there are the Chief Executive and the other paid employees of the charity – and also a President, who may take the chair at AGMs and perhaps confirm the officers of the charity in their appointments but whose other duties seem to be whatever he or she cares to undertake. One might feel that such people are (in some sense) the leading 'volunteer' of the charity. The 'bare trustees' might appear to be voluntary ambassadors, and it may be that a suitable title would be something like 'Vice President'.

However, if such people are not trustees, the body of which they are members cannot be the Council *of Trustees*. We consider the nomenclature of committees later, but for the moment we suggest that it would be logical for the Council of a charity to be the common forum for both trustees and the elected, *ex officio* and nominated representatives. This body *could* include representatives of the (non-trustee) employees and others who might be held to be 'stakeholders' in the charity, when it might be empowered to fulfil the functions of a supervisory board. However, this need not be its function in all cases.

POINTS FOR **DISCUSSION**

6h Whether it should be possible to appoint persons (who might be called 'vice presidents') to represent the charity at a senior level, who take no part in its administration and are therefore not trustees.

6i Whether it should be possible for other bodies or offices to nominate persons (who might be called 'institutional representatives') to be their representatives in the charity, without taking any part in its administration.

6j Whether it should be possible for the council of a charity to comprise both classes of representative, together with the executive and non-executive trustees of the charity.

6k Whether it should be possible for non-trustee members of council to take full part in the discussion of matters of policy, and other administrative matters such as the approval of the annual report and accounts.

6l Whether voting rights on council should be reserved to the trustees.

Experts and regional representatives

There is one other class of person to be found in some charities, whose status may be equally ambiguous. Quite a number of our respondents invite experts of various kinds to be members of their subcommittees; usually the Chair of those committees will be a trustee, as may some of the other members. In addition, the paid senior executives are often full voting members of these committees, as opposed to merely being 'in attendance' thereat. This arrangement is quite common for 'investment committees', but other technical committees often find their members in this way. Presumably these committees, or at least their non-trustee members, are not invited to set policy for the charity – as opposed to advising the trustees about it. However, there are examples among our sample where the committees do undertake executive action.

This ambiguity is compounded by the way in which these committees and their memberships are presented in annual reports. The trustees and senior officials are listed among the 'legal and administrative information', as the Charities SORP recommends; the SORP is also followed by setting out the membership of the various committees. The SORP contains no requirement to provide a separate listing of the non-trustee/non-senior official members of the committees – and it might be difficult to decide what they might be called if it did. However, it means that one can ascertain the identities of these people only by 'ticking off' the names of the trustees and senior officials in each committee!

It is not difficult to place these committee members in the scheme of things for charities. Because senior paid executives are invited to give their expertise in this way, one may suppose that the outside experts are unpaid or 'volunteer' senior executives. Their position is no different from that of other volunteers within the charity.

A final ambiguity over the nomenclature of (possible) trustees is the use by one of our respondents of the term 'regional representative', to describe a group who were not classified as trustees but emerged as a major force in the charity's Executive Committee. The issues arising from the existence of regions and branches are complex. In this case one might think that it would have been appropriate to give them trustee status in the first place but this is a classic example of an issue that can be decided only in the light of the intentions of the charity, those representatives and the people who elected them.

POINTS FOR **DISCUSSION**

6m Whether all the members of any standing committee of the charity should be listed under an appropriate category in the 'legal and administrative information' section of the annual report.

6n Whether members of such committees who are not otherwise listed as 'trustees' or 'principal officers' should be listed and described as 'senior executive volunteers'.

Persons having 'the general control, responsibility and management of the administration of a charity'

Should all members of Council be 'trustees'? Is participation in policy-making the essential mark of trusteeship? The definition in the Charities Act 1993 (as expanded in the Glossary appended to the Charities SORP) is not too clear on this matter:

> '"Trustees" are persons having the general control, responsibility and management of the administration of a charity. Custodian trustees are not within this definition.'

Clearly, mere legal ownership of the assets of a charity makes one a trustee *for* the charity, but not necessarily *of* the charity. A common expansion of this definition is on the lines of 'persons in whose hands lie the determination of the policy of the charity and the general control and management of its administration'. In short, trusteeship involves *both* policy-making *and* executive responsibilities, but may exclude the legal ownership of the charity's assets. However, this does not necessarily confine trustee status to those who are members of some specific 'executive committee', and there is an obvious role for non-executive trustees in every charity.

The general bodies of trustees in all our respondent charities commonly approve the report and accounts of their organisation. One might suppose that they do this because they can *monitor* its executive activity in sufficient detail to be able to do so. However, our research has suggested that many 'trustees' are in no position to do this in a positive way, and that they tend to follow the leadership of their finance committees, treasurers or even the external auditor in such matters. 'Trustees' who behave in this way either are neglecting their duty toward the charity or are carrying out some other function than that of trusteeship.

Legal responsibilities of trustees

Another topic we discussed with the trustees themselves was, therefore, their appreciation of the legal constraints under which they operated. How did they decide what their charity could and could not do? How aware were they of charity law or (where applicable) company law? Or of the Charity Commission or 'umbrella' bodies such as NCVO? At bottom, who is finally responsible for what is going on? We summarise in Table 5 what was said by the trustees.

TABLE 5 TRUSTEES AND THE LAW

Trustee	Constraints on activities and behaviour (in order of importance)				Trustees' knowledge of ('others' means they rely on other people)			Ultimate responsibility?
	Governing instrument	Charity law etc	Finance	Other	Charity law	Company law	Charity Commission, etc	
A	2nd	3rd	1st	–	Others	Others	Slight	Council
B	1st	–	–	–	Others	Others	Slight	Chair
C	1st	2nd	–	–	Others	Others	Others	Trustees
D	1st	–	2nd	–	Yes	Yes	Yes	Trustees
E	1st	–	–	2nd	Yes	Yes	Yes?	Trustees
F	–	2nd	–	1st	?	?	?	Chair
G	–	=1st	–	=1st	Yes	Others	Others	Chair
H	–	1st	–	2nd	Yes	?	Others	Chair
I	–	1st	–	–	Umbrella organisation	Auditor	Umbrella organisation	Trustees
				–				
J	1st	3rd	–	2nd	Slight	N/A	Yes	Board
K	1st	–	–	–	Yes	Yes	Yes	Trustees
L	1st	2nd	–	3rd	Yes	Yes	Yes	Trustees
M	–	1st	–	–	Yes	N/A	Yes	Trustees but ...
N	–	1st	–	–	Yes	Yes	No	Trustees but ...
O	–	1st	–	–	Others	Others	Others	Council
P	–	1st	–	–	Yes	Yes	Yes	Trustees

– view not expressed; ? not clear from interview

In general, one might be surprised that more trustees did not put their governing instrument, or an equivalent document, as the primary constraint on what they did. Some opted for 'the law' (for example, in the university) because of a reasonable doubt as to whether they actually have a 'governing instrument' as opposed to being directly subject to some general or even private Act of Parliament. The university's 'governor' was quite forthright:

'The members of the Board of Governors of a university usually see themselves first and foremost as "governors" and secondly (if the university is a limited company, as here) as "directors" of the company which runs it; only occasionally do they see themselves as acting as "charity trustees". It follows that they see the objectives of the university more in terms of the Education Acts than those of general charity law.'

Again it might seem odd that more trustees did not see the charity's financial resources as a major factor in what they could and could not do; perhaps they felt it was too obvious to mention. The 'other constraints' perceived by some trustees are interesting. Three suggested some variant of 'prudence' such as 'sixth sense' or 'good practice'; two considered the compatibility of the proposal of importance – 'Does it fit in with the existing work?', 'Is it something in which we can really help right away?' A sixth gave 'the wishes of the membership' equal place with the law – in first place; he added:

'The charity's constitution is not an insuperable barrier to desired action, since it can be varied – although this must take time.'

Turning to their understanding of the law, it is disturbing to see how many charity trustees rely on their paid officials or other advisers in such matters. One or two qualified this statement along the lines of:

'. . . although especially grave issues might not be suitable for such delegation by the Trustees.'

Sadly perhaps, the Charity Commission, Companies House and the various 'umbrella' organisations do not figure largely with many trustees. (A notable exception was the one who relied upon one such organisation for matters of charity and company law!) Several others seemed well acquainted with the Charity Commission, and, on the whole, those who had happy memories of the encounter were balanced by those who did not. Little purpose would be served by describing the issues of contention; without exception, they concerned the point at which a proper concern for the lawful administration of the charity might (or might not) have strayed over into issues of how the charities were to *operate*. It seemed to us that the nature of the Commission's *regulatory* role was not altogether understood by the charities – and indeed may stand in need of a clearer definition.

Finally, it can be seen that four of the sixteen trustees supposed that it was the Chair who carried ultimate responsibility for what went on. A possible excuse is that three of the four were in fact the Chair of their charity. One of the others added:

'. . . although the Chairman might have an especial duty in this respect.'

Whatever the legal position might be, it probably *would* be the Chair who would receive most of the criticism in the event of a major scandal. This possibility, that the collective responsibility of a board was not absolutely indivisible, was explained in more detail by the university governor:

'. . . it has to be borne in mind that the Vice Chancellor is a member of the Board, but also acts as the Chief Executive and the official "accounting officer" of the university. Furthermore, the responsibility of the Board of Governors for academic matters is confined to the educational character and mission of the university; the detailed responsibility is that of the Vice Chancellor and his Academic Board.'

Non-executive trustees have a duty to oversee what is going on and exercise the same care as they would in their own affairs. Nevertheless, the primary responsibility for what is happening rests with the senior *executives* of the charity, whether they are executive trustees or not.

Trustees and finance

If trustees are truly those who have 'the general control, responsibility and management of the administration of a charity', they must be able to take a view of the financial information that is placed before them. Accordingly, we led our conversations with the trustees into several topics relating to accounting, reserve policies, the auditors and general management. The responses are summarised in Table 6.

In general we accepted what the trustees said of themselves, except that we assumed that qualified accountants and bankers could probably have answered 'Yes' to the question about formal knowledge of accounting! A couple of the other respondents made interesting points about how those without formal training might see things.

'The trustee believes that he and his fellow trustees are entitled to rely on the advice of (a) the auditor(s) and (b) the paid officials with respect to all matters of accounting and internal control. He points out that these officials are not appointed by the charity; they are local government officers who are seconded by the local authority in response to a request from the charity for certain types of assistance. Moreover, the work of the paid officials is subject to inspection by the District Auditor in addition to that of the charity's own external auditor.'

TABLE 6 TRUSTEES, FINANCE AND MANAGEMENT

| Trustee | Formal knowledge of accounting | Heard of SORP etc? | Valuation vs historical cost? | Expectations of the auditor | | | Manage or monitor? |
				Detect fraud	Check on compliance	Check on systems	
A	Not detailed	Vaguely	–	Limited extent	Yes	–	Manage
B	Can follow balance sheet	No	Valuation	Yes	–	–	Manage
C	'Others'	No	–	No	Yes	–	?
D	Yes	Yes	Historical	Yes	Yes	Yes	Restricted extent
E	Yes	Partially	Historical	No	Yes	Yes	No
F	Yes	–	–	No	Yes	Yes	Yes
G	Yes	Partially	Historical ?	Not really	–	Yes	Restricted
H	Not directly	Yes	Valuation	Yes	–	Yes?	Yes
I	'Others'	–	–	Yes?	–	–	Overview
J	Yes	No	Valuation	?	?	?	–
K	Yes	Yes	Both	Yes	–	–	Both
L	Some	Partially	Valuation	No	Yes	?	–
M	Yes	Yes	Historical	?	?	?	Both
N	Not directly	Partially	Valuation	Yes	–	–	Yes
O	Can follow balance sheet	Partially	Historical	?	–	?	Restricted
P	'Illiterate'	Partially	–	?	–	–	?

– view not expressed;   ? not clear from interview

This comment needs to be considered alongside what both the trustee and the paid officials themselves said about this charity, which is a community association set up within a 'community school' – a product of 'a 1970s vision of education from the cradle to the grave, which was entertained by a number of councillors and head-teachers at that time'. The local authority and its officers are in many ways the driving force here. Also, we have noted that many other charities have people seconded to them from outside organisations for a variety of purposes: who controls such people, or takes responsibility for their actions?

Another response, which must find echoes in the way many non-accountant trustees face up to financial matters, was this:

'The trustee reckons himself to be "financially illiterate" with respect to the finer points of "generally accepted accounting principles". However, he claims a good grasp of the "financial logic" of the charity's situation, which flows from his "hands on" understanding of the organisation and its activities. (As Treasurer, he signs all cheques for amounts over £200!)'

It can be seen that most of these trustees have heard about the SORP Accounting by Charities; many were unaware that it is to be followed by regulations on the same topic. Again, a quotation will provide some deeper appreciation of how such things are seen 'at the coal-face':

'. . . these documents are somewhat "over the top", and require the charity to provide so much detail as to render its accounts very hard for the lay person to understand. The charity has not until now presented additional summarised accounts for lay people, but it is likely that this will be done in future.'

On the question of whether a charity's assets should be carried at market price or historical cost, the trustees who commented on this issue were divided 50/50 between some sort of 'valuation' and histor-ical cost. For the most part, trustees produced reasoned arguments for their choices:

'The trustee feels in favour of using valuations (as opposed to historical cost) for all assets, because they have more meaning for management purposes.'

'He has a preference for historical cost, over market value, as a method of asset valuation. Market value introduces largely meaningless fluctuations into the accounts . . .'

'NHS trusts are compelled to place market values on all their assets, in order to provide an appropriate "scenario of capital charges" for assessing their ability to cover their full costs.'

'He feels comfortable with the new proposal that investments should appear on the balance sheet at market value, with the resulting holding gains and losses being reported as investment gains. It appears as if the Charity Commission *might* be trying to make capital profits be treated as income. In an inflationary world, capital gains are necessary *to maintain* the *real* value of capital and reserves. Holding gains should therefore not be reported as income . . . With respect to the major fixed assets of this charity, he believes that the overriding requirement of its accounts is that its Income and Expenditure Account should visibly equate cash income with cash expenditure. Capitalisation and depreciation charges would result in surpluses and deficits that would disguise the underlying balance between what was raised and what was spent.'

Expectations of external auditors

On the trustees' expectations of the external auditor, those who came down one way or the other on the question of the detection of fraud by the auditor were once again divided 50/50. Many made more-or-less distinct references to matters of compliance and the effectiveness of systems of control. In general, one felt that the trustees were divided between those who had unduly high expectations of their auditors and those with comparatively few expectations at all. A few quotations give the flavour of what was said.

'The trustee expects the external auditor to check the accuracy of the accounts, and also to report on the general levels of compliance with the charity's internal regulations regarding financial matters. It follows that their ability to detect truly intelligent fraud is limited to detecting the non-compliance with regulations which makes it possible.'

'Possible dishonesty on the part of staff is the least of the Foundation's problems; this is due in part to their high quality, but also to the currently stable nature of the Foundation's activities.'

'The trustee accepts that it is the duty of the trustees themselves to put in a sound system of management and control. It follows that it is the auditor's duty to see that the records and reports correspond with the requirements of law, and also to check on levels of compliance . . .'

'. . . the internal audit is an important second line of defence, and there is a comprehensive policy of separating sensitive tasks within the charity, as far as staff numbers allow.'

'He does not look to them for any significant financial advice, nor does he suppose that they would be able to detect a well-concealed fraud.'

'The trustee expects the external auditors to supply general advice over financial matters, check that everything is in order, and flag up any problems. They should at least have an inkling if a major fraud has taken place.'

'The Trust is audited by the District Auditor. The trustee feels that this quite costly matter can be dealt with most effectively if the District Auditor evaluates the work of the Trust's own Internal Audit Section, and allows the compliance testing to be dealt with by [them] . . . He also feels that there tends to be some confusion over the role of the Audit Committee. It is not part of the audit process itself, neither does it carry out the functions of a fully fledged Finance Committee.'

'The trustee believes that the auditor's duty is (1) to confirm the accuracy of the accounts and records, (2) to ensure the appropriate presentation of the accounts, and (3) to warn the charity of danger areas, especially with respect to VAT and other forms of taxation. However, there is an overriding duty to counter opportunities for substantial fraud . . .'

'He has no great confidence in their ability to detect and correct errors and frauds.'

'The trustee expects the external auditors to keep a very close eye on every aspect of the charity's financial affairs – which is what they are paid to do!'

'He thinks the auditor ought to be able to find out if any money is missing.'

'The trustee expects the external auditors to detect and correct all errors, and hopes that they would detect frauds, unless they involved forgery and misstatements of considerable ingenuity. He also expects a reasonable amount of financial advice as part of the audit service.'

Trustees and general management

Most trustees seemed to feel that the question of whether trustees should take part in the general management of the charity was a major problem:

'The day-to-day management of the operations of the Foundation are clearly the province of the paid officials, within policies laid down by the trustees. However, the actual grant-making process is more in the hands of the trustees themselves.'

'The charity's operations are both large scale and increasingly "hi-tech", and therefore best left in the hands of carefully chosen professional managers. Non-executives have to be careful not to involve themselves in these technical details, but to concentrate on the provision of policy.'

'The trustee feels that charity trustees should pay some attention to matters of "routine" management as well as issues of policy and planning. They need to be sure that the paid officials are doing their jobs properly.'

'Trustees "have to balance on a tight-rope" between ensuring a hands-on appreciation of what is happening and giving the paid officials proper scope for initiative.'

'The Board has a duty to advise the Vice Chancellor on the management of the university, so an understanding of the general principles of management is fundamental to its work. However, "executive management" is the function of the Vice Chancellor and his staff.'

'An understanding of the general principles of management . . . is fundamental to the "financial logic" needed to control the charity's activities.'

Whether or not trustees are truly aware of the fact, they are required to set up and maintain proper systems of control over the activities of their charity. All our respondent charities had some system in operation, although it was not always enshrined in a formal manual of regulations and procedures. Our objective was to discuss with the trustees how they believed that they 'stayed on top of the situation' in their charities. Table 7 summarises their replies.

In general, our trustees seemed satisfied with their external auditor, although occasionally satisfaction was grudging:

'. . . the external auditor does a good job but his effectiveness is limited. This is because most opportunities for fraud occur at branch level. Each branch has an auditor, who must be a qualified person but need not be in professional practice . . .'

'. . . he may fairly be described as "all we've got".'

'The trustee believes that the external audit should provide a major defence against losses.'

'. . . the external auditors do a good job, as evidenced by their continued re-election.'

'. . . the auditor does a good job but his effectiveness is limited by the fact that he must maintain his independence – and so operate at a certain distance from

TABLE 7 HOW TRUSTEES KNOW WHAT IS GOING ON

Trustee	Rating of external auditor?	Specific examples of controls?	Control system generally?	Reliance on others for control?	Reliance on budgetary control?	Insurance matters?
A	OK	Yes	–	Yes	–	Occasionally
B	Others	–	Not discussed	–	–	Chair
C	–	–	Not discussed	–	–	–
D	–	–	–	–	–	–
E	OK	–	Discussed	–	–	–
F	OK	–	Aware	–	–	Others
G	Good?	Yes	Reviewed	Yes	Yes	Others
H	Rely on	–	–	–	Yes	–
I	OK	–	–	Yes	–	Often
J	Could do better	–	Approved	–	–	Major concern
K	–	–	–	Yes	–	–
L	–	–	Not seen	Yes	Yes	Not major, but …
M	OK	Yes	Discussed	–	–	Others
N	Assume OK	–	–	Yes?	Yes	Very important
O	OK	–	–	Yes	–	Frequently
P	Assume OK	Yes	–	*Reverse!*	–	Confident

? not clear from interview

the organisation . . . [The trustee] has greatest confidence in the application of internal control within the accounts department itself.'

Control systems

With reference to one or more control devices, several of our respondents mentioned specific items:

'. . . the control system . . . contains a list of approved signatories.'

'. . . the trustee himself, as Deputy Chairman, signs all cheques over £500 . . .'

and Trustee N signs all those over £200.

A rather distressing number of trustees seemed to know little of their control systems, and rarely discussed the matter:

'The trustee is aware of the existence of a formal manual of procedures for the organisation, but its contents are never fully discussed as a matter of routine. Substantial changes in the scope of the authority of some official or post will be discussed, and the opportunity may be taken to remind Trustees of the existing situation.'

'Every trustee is given a full copy of the Regulations in force. However, they are not compelled to read them, and the issues of internal control involved are rarely, if ever, discussed. Nevertheless, they are looked at when major changes occur . . .'

'. . . the trustee is aware of the "Authorisation Procedures" covering the activities of the Finance Department. These are reviewed from time to time by the Committee.'

'The trustee is not aware of the precise details of the control systems operating within the charity . . . he would hope that the external auditor, the Treasurer, the Chief Executive and the Finance Director will have satisfied themselves over its details.'

It is also rather disturbing to see how many trustees in addition to this last one do seem to rely on other people, even other agencies, to oversee the control systems in their charities. On the other hand, responsibility is not absolute or indivisible, and trustees are surely entitled to suppose that Finance Directors and Treasurers 'have an especial concern for all financial issues' – but not to the exclusion of their own critical faculties:

' The trustee is not sure of the precise nature of the control systems operating within the Finance Directorate of the charity . . . Trustees are entitled to rely upon the Hon. Treasurer to oversee these matters more closely . . .'

'. . . Of course, the honorary treasurers have an especial concern for all financial issues concerning the charity; other trustees must place a certain confidence in their ability to spot and pursue unusual events.'

'The trustee supposes that the control systems operating within the charity are a matter of "custom and practice". Financial matters are largely under the control of the paid officials; because they are all local government officers, he believes that it is incumbent on them to follow procedures, under their contracts of employment with the local authority – whose responsibility it is to see that they observe them.'

'It is the job of the Director of Finance and the external auditor to alert trustees to any deficiencies. The trustee feels that as a group they are reasonably streetwise and alert. One can't be complacent, so it may be that the trustees themselves should be more watchful in its area . . .'

'Subsidiary lines of defence are . . . (2) the Audit Committee . . . (3) the system of quality audit and performance review applied to the management of the charity – to which must be added advice on various specific matters of security from the charity's solicitors and the Bank of England; (4) ensuring the engagement of competent and reliable senior staff, and making sure that they understand and comply with internal control and guidelines.'

'The trustee assumes that the financial regulations approved by both the internal auditors and external auditors are efficient . . .'

The other side of the coin comes from a treasurer:

'Finally, the trustee is conscious that, because he is the treasurer, other members of the NEC (and the membership generally), largely rely on him to control financial matters on their behalf. As has been said, people tend to place the same reliance on the other "chairs". In the trustee's view, it is important that this reliance should be placed in the person's office rather than in their personal experience in accountancy – or being black or female. Trustees should not pontificate on the basis of personal specialism (even if they have it) but be at pains to exercise due diligence as a lay person, on behalf of other lay people.'

All our respondent charities (save one) have both budgets and interim management accounts, and it would seem that these are all presented to at least some of the trustees and are the object of extensive discussion and enquiry. However, only five trustees seemed to make a specific reference to these procedures as a part of 'how we know we are not being robbed'. It may be that the others are less aware of the preventive purpose of the exercise and just see it as part of the general monitoring of the charity's activities.

'For the rest, she considers the setting of budgets and the comparison of budgets with actual performance to be the best form of control that a trustee can exercise. In this respect, she considers that the trustee's intuitive knowledge of the financial implications of what is going on is of the essence.'

'More generally, the charity's security depends on four lines of defence, in the following order: (1) the system of budgetary control and management reporting of variances etc; . . .'

Insurance

Finally, some people have commented on the lack of concern among trustees for insurance matters. All our respondents seemed to be aware of the issue, although again quite a few saw it as a matter for others to deal with.

'The trustee supposes that matters of insurance cover and the safeguarding of assets must be his own primary responsibility, as Chairman. However, he has never seen the insurance policies themselves.'

'Matters of insurance cover (in the widest sense) are a major concern within an NHS trust. There is a special Risk Management Committee charged with these and other issues. It should be noted that, as part of the NHS changes, hospitals have lost Crown immunity, and the future, bearing in mind a more litigious environment, is uncertain indeed.'

'. . . there have been some difficulties with the Charity Commissioners over the matter of negligence cover for the trustees.'

This last quotation encapsulates the culture clashes that are becoming more and more frequent within the voluntary sector. The charity in question is the one that operates banking and investment services for other charities and their donors, and the traditional idea of a charity does not really allow for the not-for-profit business.

In a general way, it might seem undesirable that trustees should insure against their personal liability for negligence and charge the premiums against charitable funds. However, in a high technology activity carried out in an increasingly litigious environment, it is by no means obvious what some judge and jury (perhaps in a foreign jurisdiction) might decide, or award, against the trustees. Perhaps it would be helpful if normal 'limited liability' could apply to charities; maybe the 'regulation' of such issues is in truth a highly technical matter, better handled by a specialist agency.

Summary and issues

All our respondents took some steps to acquaint newly appointed trustees with the general nature of their duties, charity law etc. Sometimes this was no more than giving them a package of literature about the charity, plus some other material from the NCVO, Charity Commission and so on. Another common feature of the process was an interview with the Chief Executive, and this sometimes extended to quite elaborate 'induction courses'. The purpose of such interviews or 'courses' was not all one-way; they were often seen as opportunities for the charity to discover the particular interests and strengths of the new trustee.

A few charities commenced the process with the nomination of candidates for trusteeship, who were also sent copies of the regulations etc, and even required them to sign to the effect that they understood what might be required of them. At least one charity made the actual induction into a little ceremony, concluding with the new trustee's signature of the minute book confirming the appointment. Other respondents were running courses for *existing* trustees. This seems a necessary step, given the changing nature of the voluntary sector; less happily, many of the others seemed to place considerable reliance on their trustees' previous experience as volunteers or as trustees of other charities.

Although at least one respondent put on courses for its volunteers, none seemed to extend this type of instruction to their paid staff – or their professional advisers. This was remarkable given the degree of reliance that several of the trustees claimed to place on such people's knowledge of these matters! The general public is clearly not aware that voluntary sector matters occupy at best a negligible part of the syllabus – and examinations – of most professional accounting bodies.

Nevertheless, even when the professional advisers are well versed in charity law and company law, it remains essential for all trustees at least to be aware of what they need to ask their advisers to do! An earlier research project has suggested that many small charities do not have their companies-limited-by-guarantee properly maintained because of their ignorance.

POINTS FOR DISCUSSION

7a Whether charities should take steps to ensure that all candidates for trusteeship fully understand the nature of the duties and responsibilities they have offered to undertake.

7b Whether charities should provide some formal induction process to consolidate this understanding in newly appointed trustees.

7c Whether these processes should be seen by both the charity and the trustee as the first step in an on-going process of continuing education in charity matters.

7d Whether suitable instruction in relevant aspects of charity law and procedures should be given to all voluntary workers, especially those with executive or fundraising responsibilities.

7e Whether participation in all these educational opportunities (or a parallel programme) should be mandatory for any members of the paid staff of the charity who play any part in its administrative processes.

7f Whether charities should ensure, as far as possible, that their professional advisers and their staffs have engaged in suitable courses of professional education on charity matters.

CHAPTER EIGHT

Nomenclature of committees

In addition to the meeting of the trustees as a body, all our charities, save one, also have one or more subcommittees. This information is presented in Table 8 but, again, it does not give a full account of the diversity of practice that exists.

Types and numbers of committees

It can be seen from Table 8 that some of our charities operate through an executive committee, and others do not. However, even this apparently simple observation requires qualification, for a reason that very well illustrates the diversity of terminology as well as of practice to be found in the governance of the voluntary sector. Charities 4, 5, 7, 8 and 13 do not have an executive committee as such but the bodies shown against them in the 'Finance Committee' column actually bear the respective titles 'General Purposes and Finance Committee', 'Finance and Establishment Committee', 'Finance and General Purposes Committee', 'Resources Committee' and 'Budgetary Control Committee'. It is probable that these committees have a wider remit than that of a simple finance committee but the distinction is not altogether clear.

Table 8 also shows those charities that have audit committees and investment advisory committees. In general, an audit committee should consist of non-executives and have direct access to the main Board or Council of the charity. In Charities 1 and 14 there is no intervening finance committee or executive committee. Charity 6 has no finance committee, and the distinctly 'executive' nature of its executive committee has been a matter of comment; some common memberships of the two committees might be felt to weaken its effectiveness. In Charities 9 and 16 the Audit Committee reports to the Finance Committee; and in Charities 1, 6 and 16 paid officials are in attendance at the meetings.

TABLE 8 NOMENCLATURE AND ANNUAL FREQUENCY OF COMMITTEE MEETINGS

Charity	Main Board	Executive Committee	Finance Committee	Audit Committee	Investment Advisory Committee	Appointments/ Nominations Committee	Salaries/ Remuneration Committee	Others (number only)
1	12	-	-	4	Occasional	Occasional	Occasional	12
2	6	-	-	-	-	-	-	0
3	2	4	4	-	3/4	-	-	8
4	4/5	-	4/5	-	-	-	-	8/10
5	5	-	4/6	-	-	-	-	4
6	4	4	-	4	4	-	-	3+
7	4	-	6	-	-	-	-	2+
8	6	-	6	3	-	-	2	2
9	4	6	6	Occasional	3	Occasional	-	1+14
10	5	-	-	-	2	-	-	6
11	4	12	-	-	-	-	-	1
12	3	5	2/3	-	-	-	2/3	6
13	8	-	12	-	4	-	-	6
14	8	-	-	4	-	-	1+	Several
15	2	12	-	-	Occasional	-	Occasional	Ad hoc
16	4	9	9	6/8	6/8	-	6/8	5
17	3	-	3	3	-	3	3	2+3
18	1	5	-	-	-	-	-	0

- no such committee

Several of our respondents (Charities 2, 3, 5, 7, 12 and 15) have no audit committee but their auditors make similar personal presentations of the accounts and the content of their management letters etc to either the finance committee or the full Council. Charity 10 has no such committee as a matter of policy, as has been mentioned, while at Charity 5:

'The Trustees' Meeting has formally decided against the appointment of an Audit Committee, on the grounds that the matter is too important to be delegated to a further subcommittee. In fact, all the trustees are invited to attend the meeting of the Finance and Establishment Committee, which discusses the audited accounts with the auditors.'

The trustee interviewed from Charity 7 made a comment on the practice of having staff members present at such meetings:

'He feels that a face-to-face meeting with the auditors . . . without the Finance Officer in attendance, would be pointless "because of the obscure jargon which auditors tend to use".'

Charity 18 has no audit committee because the 'real' accounts are prepared and audited at branch level, and then consolidated for the regional and national levels above them.

Three of our respondents have an Appointments or Nominations Committee that searches for and nominates candidates for trustee-ship. Seven have a Salaries or Remuneration Committee that deals with the pay of senior paid officials and sometimes with that of other staff.

Table 8 also gives the number of other committees maintained by these charities. Some of these committees are functional, dealing with activities such as personnel and public relations; others are dis-ciplinary, in the sense that they deal with different sections of the charitable activities. Yet others are regional, and deal with specific parts of the country or countries in which the charity operates. Several respondents reported ad hoc working parties, in addition. Our respondent from Charity 12 set out the typical arrangements with respect to these committees:

'The standing committees consist of between two and six trustees, together with other non-trustee members, appointed by the Executive Committee, to cover the various areas of concern to the charity such as . . . , . . . and finance. They act in a purely advisory capacity to the Executive Committee, which takes most decisions in these matters unless it specifically delegates responsibility to the relevant standing committee. Members are appointed to serve for ten years, but are required to stand down for at least one year thereafter. In addition, there is a Technical Advisory Group, whose members are distinguished scientists and engineers, and not often trustees at all . . . There are also some working parties, notably a Salaries Working Party . . .'

Notable aspects

A few matters are worthy of comment, discussed below.

Numbers of committees

Charity 1 has sixteen committees over all, and Charity 9 has no fewer than twenty. The former is the NHS trust where there is a very clear directive for open governance, hence the formidable number of committees, and we have referred to the quantities of paperwork that they generate. The explanation for Charity 16's count is its fourteen regional committees.

Subsidiary companies

Charity 6 differs from the other charities in that it includes the boards of directors of its subsidiary companies in the list of subcommittees of its Executive Committee. This is particularly appropriate because the subsidiaries in question operate its principal charitable activities – as a bank and an investment trust – rather than as the traditional fundraising 'trading company'. In fact, three other respondents have companies that carry out some part of their charitable activity.

This charity no doubt finds it convenient to ring-fence the regulatory activities of the Bank of England in this way. One of the other charities had a very different reason for creating its company:

'Its purpose is to establish the difference between "free" services to members, under the terms of their subscriptions, and additional items for which specific payment is required.'

In another case, the small company was a useful device to obtain a licence to operate a passenger aircraft in East Africa. All the remaining charities have trading companies and five of the charities are themselves companies-limited-by-guarantee. One might reflect that the principal reason for the creation of almost all these companies is the difficulty of transferring assets and executing agreements with an unincorporated entity. A secondary reason is that trading is not a charitable activity and the Inland Revenue taxes any profits arising in this way; this can be recovered by passing the activity to a company, which covenants to pay its profits over to the charity.

Only three of our respondents do not have any non-charitable companies. There is little to comment on them, except the points that have already been mentioned: (1) several of them do not engage in 'fundraising' trading but actually perform part of the charitable work itself; and (2) two charities consider the boards of directors of their companies to be subcommittees of the charity itself. Those boards commonly consist of a mixture of trustees and senior paid officials. Three include 'outsiders' and one consists solely of paid officials of the charity. No salaries or other remuneration is paid to any trustee directors of these companies.

Pension funds

Two of our charities make reference to their pension funds in their lists of committees. Clearly, these are always separate trusts from the employing charity but, as Charity 15 observed:

'. . . all such schemes represent a major source of expenditure for the charities that have them – and could prove a very serious drain indeed if they were ever found to be underfunded.'

Attendance at meetings

All our respondents classed attendance by trustees at meetings as pretty good, at least in the case of the 'real' elected trustees; that of the nominated and *ex officio* members is less good in many cases – but not all. Two charities consider attendance figures as part of formal assessments of 'committee efficiency'; several others make a note of absentees, who eventually receive a letter from the Chair enquiring as to whether they can really spare the time . . .'

Family/business connections

None of the respondents reported any notable business or family connections between their trustees – except for the one in which three-quarters of the trustees are required to be blood relatives of the founder. However, several of the more high-profile charities referred to apparently long-standing personal friendships among certain sections of their trustees:

'. . . however, not a few could be said to be well acquainted, as they move in a comparatively limited social group.'

'. . . however, the Ordinary Trustees were originally chosen for their close ties with the founder and his company.'

'However, since they are selected as a result of being "known" to other trustees, rather than by direct nomination, a number would appear to have long-standing associations outside the charity.' [The trustees from this charity confirmed that they had been introduced to its activities through membership of a sporting club, whose activities impinged on those of the charity.]

Conflict of interest

A majority of the sample have specific policies requiring the disclosure of conflicts of interest; both they and the charities without such policies reported comparatively rare occasions when trustees either have withdrawn or refrained from voting on these grounds. Some of their observations are relevant:

'In a general way, the presence of a number of medical consultants in the specialism that is the subject of the charity's objectives may give some scope for such conflicts, but the charity does not make research grants of any kind.'

'Nevertheless, several of the trustees are engaged in business ventures and professional practices that are closely connected with the work of the charity, and considerable care is needed to prevent such conflicts arising.'

'However, the nature of the charity is such that a number of its trustees are likely to be local government officers, with the same authorities as those with whom the charity must "deal" . . .'

'This may be considered the "up side" of the non-democratic selection methods referred to above; [people] with existing or conceivable financial interests in the charity's operations are excluded from nomination.'

'This is a charity whose objects often arouse strong feelings among its supporters; there are some grounds for supposing that a few members [of the Board] may not have fully disclosed their interests in other organisations.'

'. . . a number of trustees are also branch officers, and some conflicts can arise from this.'

Summary and issues

One might suppose that the charities with a specific executive committee will be those with more than about fifteen trustees in all, who might otherwise experience difficulty in reducing the broad principles of policy to a more detailed plan of action by reason of the numbers present. As Charities 5 and 7 do not have very large numbers of trustees, there could be grounds for supposing that the committees just described are likely to act principally as 'finance committees'.

Comparison of Table 2 with Table 8 shows that the correlation between number of trustees and the use of an executive committee would seem to hold in fourteen cases. However, there are four exceptions: 4, 6, 11 and 13. Charity 4 is interesting in several ways: it is a broadly based organisation in which the various committees act with a considerable degree of independence. In Charity 6, in which a twelve-strong Board of Trustees delegates some of its powers to a four-strong Executive Committee, the composition of this subcommittee is the Chairman plus three other trustees, with the full 'management team' (the Director and the four senior managers) in attendance. Charity 6 is one of the more technically involved charities in our sample: it is the umbrella charity that is operating as a financial institution. One might suppose that, in this case, it might be necessary for some of the trustees to work much more closely with the senior managers than is required to run a less-involved charity. In short, this charity is probably very near to the 'commercial model'. It is a not-for-profit business and the trustees who are members of *this* Executive Committee are effectively (volunteer) executive directors, while the remaining trustees perform the role of non-executive directors. This can be compared with the arrangement at the NHS trust, which also operates a technically involved activity. Here there are five 'non-executive directors' plus the Chairman, who sit together on the trust Board with the five 'executive directors'. Presumably the role of an executive committee is fulfilled by the executive directors. At Charity 11, a twelve-strong Council of Management delegates power to a three-strong Executive Committee, which meets monthly. This arrangement may compensate for the small number of full-time staff at this charity. The comparative frequency of the meetings of the main board of Charity 13 may explain their ability to dispense with an executive committee.

Again, one might suppose that any executive committee would meet more frequently than the full Board of Trustees but this is not the case with Charity 6, where both meet on the same number of occasions. As this charity appears to be run on largely commercial lines, it is entirely in keeping that the executive body should have the same number of meetings as the non-executive one. This is also true for Charity 1 (the NHS trust), although this is not shown in Table 8: the executive directors have monthly meetings, as does the full Board (of which they are, of course, full members).

Another reasonable supposition would be that an executive committee would be of a manageable size, say fewer than twelve people. This assumption is correct except in the cases of Charity 9, which has a 30-strong Executive Committee, and Charity 16, which has one numbering fourteen. The situation at Charity 9 may be explained by the composition of its Executive Committee:

'. . . which currently has 30 members, plus the Director General. There are twelve elected members of Council, including the Chairman and his deputy, fourteen Chairs of Regional Committees, three appointed members of Council and three other co-opted members (two MPs and the Director General).'

It will be remembered from Table 2 that this charity has no fewer than 52 members of Council, of whom 26 are appointed members and 26 are elected members. The 'Other committees' column of Table 8 reads '1+14'; the latter number represents fourteen regional committees, each one headed by a Chair. It might be supposed that here the Executive Committee exists to produce a body with a notably different balance from the main Council: the elected members now outnumber the appointed members, whilst the regional chairs and the Director General become full members of a senior committee.

The slightly over-sized Executive Committee in Charity 16 is probably explained by that charity's declared policy of severely restricting any delegation of its Council's authority to subcommittees, combined with very detailed control over the proceedings of the other (purely advisory) bodies. Thus:

'It should be noted that all the minutes of all the advisory committees go to the Executive Committee for examination.'

And the respondent trustee for Charity 16 testified to the fact that this examination is by no means perfunctory. It would seem that a major part of the work of this Executive Committee is to screen and condense the formidable quantities of documentation, which this policy would otherwise cause to descend on the Council.

It would be hard to escape the conclusion that the charities in our sample that have substantial numbers of nominated and *ex officio* trustees on their Councils take steps to reduce their direct influence on the charities' affairs. In the cases of Charities 9 and 16, one might suppose that their over-size Executive Committees are more akin to 'shadow councils', with their other subcommittees reporting directly to them.

However, there are other charities in the sample in which the *voting* power of nominated and *ex officio* members of Council is reduced. In Charity 15, in which there are nine nominated trustees and nine *ex officio* trustees out of a total of 23, this issue is also addressed through the composition of the Executive Committee. Here the bias toward the elected members (known as 'local members') is more marked still, although the result (in a rather smaller charity) is a manageably sized committee:

'The Executive Committee consists of the Chairman, and seven other trustees (including the five local trustees) . . .'

It might seem that in such cases the executive committees are the effective principal bodies of trustees. The full councils take on something akin to the role of a joint meeting of a continental two-tier board of a company, which gives the advisory members an opportunity to make their views known without directly being able to control policy.

Finally, although this charity operates without an executive committee, the ten nominated representatives in Charity 4 have no votes at all and it might be noted that the 30 regional representatives are full members of the Council of that charity.

Especially where the trustees are (in some sense) elected by a membership, the charities with the larger bodies of trustees might be expected to adopt a structure along the lines of a local authority, for example. In such a case, one might expect the executive committee to take on the role of a cabinet, and be made up of the Chair, any deputy chairs, and the chairs of other, functional, subcommittees. This is the case with Charities 3 and 12.

However, Charities 4, 9, 13 and 16 have these characteristics but do not seem to operate in this way. Charity 4 does not have an executive committee (unless its ambiguously titled General Purposes and Finance Committee has this function). Charities 9, 13 and 16 have Executive Committees, but these do not consist solely of the chairs of other committees (although some or all of these chairs may be members, nevertheless).

Table 8 shows that eight of the eighteen charities do not have a finance committee. The commercial style of governance at Charities 1 and 6 may make this unnecessary in their case: their (not-for-profit) businesses are self-financing, so the financial dimension is present in every decision they make. This is the case for Charity 15 as well: heritage/museums are not commonly seen as businesses but they have no substantial endowments, subscription income or core-funding from outside sources: they pay their way from what they can 'earn'.

This also applies to Charity 10, which is a grant-making foundation. It does not trade, even on a not-for-profit basis, but it clearly generates its finances from its own internal resources. Thus:

'There is no Executive Committee, Finance Committee or Audit Committee, as a matter of deliberate policy.'

The slightly different but still pervasive financial dimension in this charity is described in these terms:

'The comparatively stable and long-term nature of the Foundation's activities make it more useful to adopt an 'actuarial' view of its financial situation – much as in the case of a pension fund.'

Charity 18 is also self-financing at branch level and would have no need of a specific finance committee; of course, it has no committees at all at national level, other than its Executive Committee, by reason of its aggressively 'federal' nature. In fact, there are substantial 'national' issues of a financial nature which are dealt with by that committee, but they are probably not sufficiently detailed to require a separate committee to consider them. The reason for the absence of a finance committee in Charity 2 is equally self-evident: this is a small local charity with no subcommittees at all, nor presumably any need for them. Charity 11 has a Fundraising Committee, which may fulfil many of the purposes of a formal finance committee.

This is no less significant an issue than the titles given to trustees; whilst the title given to a charity's committee no more defines its legal status than that given to one of its members, it is equally likely to mislead those who have dealings with them and even the members themselves.

It will be recollected that two of our sample of charities had very large numbers of *ex officio* and nominated representative 'trustees', comprising their (respective) Council of Trustees and Meeting of Guardians and Trustees. In reality, the composition of their executive committees greatly reduced, and in one case eliminated, the representation of the non-elected members. In another case there is no certainty that all members of its Committee of Management will be given any opportunity to administer the charity at all. We have recommended that people either act as trustees or they should not be called trustees. In the same way, it seems desirable that a meeting exclusively comprising the whole body of trustees should have a name that is not readily confused with any high-level forum at which senior non-trustees meet with the trustees.

POINTS FOR **DISCUSSION**

8a Whether any meeting comprising the whole body of trustees, but excluding any non-trustees, should be called 'the Board of Trustees'.

8b Whether the title 'Council' should be confined to committees comprising both trustees and representatives.

Some of the other titles used in the committee structure of many charities present similar ambiguities. The term 'Executive Committee' had a number of different meanings, even in our rather small sample. As has been said, in some cases it would appear to be the *real* Board of Trustees, whereas in others it was truly a *committee* of executives (paid and unpaid). Again, it is sometimes an inner Cabinet of committee chairs. In at least one case it acted as a filter for the very substantial quantities of minutes and other paperwork directed to the Council. Many charities do not have an executive committee, sometimes because size or other considerations lead them to take the business straight to the Council or Board of Trustees.

The use of a title that includes the word 'executive' must suggest that the Council or Board of Trustees has delegated some executive authority to that committee. In fact, it was rarely if ever clear from their titles what authority had been delegated to any subcommittee in our sample. In one case, authority was rarely delegated at all and then only for specific purposes. Quite a few charities described all or some of their 'disciplinary' or 'sectional' committees as being advisory only; this was especially likely when the membership included senior executive volunteers.

We emphasise that the basic requirement is self-knowledge. It is far more important that any committee knows what its function may be than that some standard names be attached to them. Appropriate names can be expected to flow from a proper understanding of their functions but it might help if more uniform, descriptive titles for some typical committees were adopted.

POINTS FOR **DISCUSSION**

8c Whether the title 'Executive Committee' should be reserved for a committee that consists solely of paid and unpaid executive trustees.

8d Whether a committee comprising the Chair of the charity and the chairs of its subcommittees should be known as 'the Committee of Chairs'.

8e Whether a committee that consolidates materials on behalf of the Council might simply be referred to as 'the Sub-council'.

8f Whether the title of every committee should clearly indicate the nature of its remit.

8g Whether purely advisory committees should include that word in their titles.

Another source of confusion, at least to outsiders, may be the use of names such as 'Finance and General Purposes Committee' and the like; a 'general purpose' is somewhat all-embracing! It seems to be used to describe what may well be a simple executive committee, committee of chairs or even a finance committee. The practice seems common in organisations that one might not expect to have need of a purely financial subcommittee, because of their self-financing nature and consequent commercial form of governance. We believe that a true finance committee is likely to be found only in budget-financing charities.

POINT FOR **DISCUSSION**

8h Whether any words added to the title 'Finance Committee' should clearly indicate the scope of its remit.

CHAPTER NINE

Servicing committee meetings

All human organisations necessarily involve more or less formal meetings. This is especially the case with those that operate on co-operative rather than authoritarian principles. They consume a good deal of time and effort, both from the members and from the administrative machine itself. 'Servicing meetings' involves the physical arrangements for the meeting, together with providing an agenda and papers for the meeting, taking and circulating the minutes, and following up on the implementation of any resolutions made by the meeting.

Who is responsible for what

This work can be carried out in a diffused way where, say, meetings of the Finance Committee are serviced by the Director of Finance and his or her staff, whilst meetings of the Executive Committee are the responsibility of the Chief Executive and his or her personal assistant. However, these agendas and minutes provide a lot of information of what is being thought and done in the organisation, and many organisations attempt to centralise the work as a useful way of 'keeping one's finger on the pulse'. Our charities provide examples of a range of ways of doing this, summarised in Table 9.

The Chief Executive is considered to be the 'relevant officer' for the Board and the Executive Committee, and all agendas are agreed in consultation with the relevant chair.

The 'special officers' have a variety of titles such as 'Trustees' Secretary', 'Clerk to the Governors' or 'Administrator'; in several cases, they service only the principal committees.

Of the four charities that reported no specific centralisation in these matters, Charity 2 has no subcommittees at all, whilst Charity 18 is the 'federal' organisation in which the 'relevant officers' at each level service the meetings at those levels. As for Charity 4:

TABLE 9 SERVICING MEETINGS

Charity	Agendas by relevant officers	Minutes by relevant officers	Agendas by Chief Executive	Agendas by special officers	Minutes by special officers	Notes
1	–	Yes	Board	Yes	–	–
2	Board	Board	–	–	–	No committees
3	Yes	Yes	–	–	–	Agendas approved by Chief Executive
4	Yes	Yes	–	–	–	–
5	Yes	–	–	–	Yes	–
6	In part	In part	–	Board and Executive	Board and Executive	–
7	Yes	In part	–	–	Board	–
8	In part	In part	–	Board and main committees	Board and main committees	–
9	In part	In part	–	Board and main committees	Board and main committees	–
10	Plus Chief Executive's p/a	Yes	–	–	–	–
11	–	–	–	Yes	Yes	–
12	Yes	–	–	–	Yes	–
13	Yes	Yes	–	–	–	–
14	–	–	–	Yes	Yes	–
15	–	–	Yes	–	Yes	–
16	–	In part	–	Yes	Board and Executive	–
17	–	–	–	Yes	Yes	–
18	Yes	Yes	–	–	–	At all levels

'. . . the functional and disciplinary committees are seen to be largely autonomous, so comment at Council is confined to matters of co-ordinating their activities within the objects of the charity.'

This may also be true of Charity 13, which resembles Charity 4 in several other respects.

Summary and issues

This last issue recalls an outwardly unrelated matter from our survey. Both a trustee and a more junior paid official commented on the incredible workload imposed on the Chief Executive in many charities. In part this may be due to his or her being the only paid trustee (where that is the case), but there seem to be two more general reasons for this overload. In many trust instruments, 'the Master', 'the Warden' and so on is the only paid official who is mentioned, together with some indication that subordinate staff may be employed, and so trustees feel that any communication to junior levels must pass through this named Chief Executive.

A more powerful reason could be that many charities have a very considerable number of committees, and the Chief Executive or his or her deputy often see it as their duty to attend at them all, and even to be involved with the preparation of the agendas. Both practices have something to commend them; given the substantial involvement of 'part-timers' at all levels in a charity, it must seem essential for some one person (or his or her deputy) to keep a hold on all the threads.

However, the effect is probably to spread these officers' attention a little too thinly in many cases, and we have observed a possible alternative method of centralising committee activity in a less damaging fashion. A number of our respondents employ a specifically nominated person, with a title such as 'Committee Secretary' or 'Clerk to the Governors', who takes instructions and sends out agendas, keeps and circulates minutes, chases up the implementation of resolutions, and so on. This official is usually a senior administrator with sufficient authority to pursue issues of this sort, and it seems that the appointment can relieve more senior people from attendance.

POINT FOR DISCUSSION

9a Whether, where a charity has a considerable number of committees to be serviced, a reasonably senior 'committee clerk' should be appointed for the purpose.

CHAPTER TEN

Auditing and financial management

Table 10 presents details of the auditors of our respondent charities.

TABLE 10 TYPES AND LENGTH OF SERVICE OF AUDITORS

Charity	District Auditor	Local firm(s)	'Big 6'	'Division A'	Time out of mind	20+ years	6–19 years	1–5 years
1	Yes	–	–	–	–	–	–	✓
2	–	Yes	–	–	–	✓	–	–
3	–	–	Yes	–	–	–	✓	–
4	–	–	–	Yes	–	✓	–	–
5	–	–	–	Yes	–	–	–	✓
6	–	–	Yes	–	–	–	–	✓
7	–	–	–	Yes	–	–	–	✓
8	–	–	–	Yes	✓	–	–	–
9	–	–	Yes	–	✓	–	–	–
10	–	–	–	Yes	✓	–	–	–
11	–	–	–	Yes	–	–	✓	–
12	–	–	Yes	–	–	✓	–	–
13	–	–	Yes	–	–	–	–	✓
14	–	–	Yes	–	✓	–	–	–
15	–	–	Yes	–	–	✓	–	–
16	–	–	–	Yes	✓	–	–	–
17	–	–	Yes	–	–	–	–	✓
18	–	Yes	–	–	✓	–	–	–

The financial governance of charities is a topic that involves the interface of the trustees, the auditors and the 'control system' operating within the charity. All charities are different, so the precise nuances of what was said about them by their spokespersons are at once of significance but somewhat confusing. Table 11 attempts a summary of what can be observed of this in our respondents but the concepts are not easily captured in the 'yes/no' format inherent in tabular presentation.

TABLE 11 AUDITORS AND TRUSTEES

Charity	Auditor face to face with	'Management letter' sent to	Prior meeting with Honorary Treasurer	Meeting with internal auditor
1	Board	Board	N/A	No
2	Board	No	Yes	No internal auditor
3	Finance Committee	Senior treasurer	Yes?	No internal auditor
4	No?	Not always	Yes	No internal auditor
5	Board	Executive Committee/Board	No?	Yes
6	Audit Committee	Finance Director	No	No
7	No?	No	No	No
8	Audit Committee	Audit Committee	No	No?
9	Audit Committee	Audit Committee	No?	Yes
10	No	Finance Director	No	No internal auditor
11	No?	None	No	No internal auditor
12	Treasurer	Yes	Yes	No internal auditor
13	Budget Committee	Budget Committee	No?	No internal auditor
14	Audit Committee	Chair	No?	Yes
15	Executive Committee	No	No	No internal auditor
16	Audit Committee	Audit Committee	No	No?
17	Audit Committee	Board via Audit Committee	No	Yes
18	Regional company	Officers	No	No internal auditor

? not clear from interview

Presentation of accounts

As can be seen in Table 11, most charity auditors do make a personal presentation of the accounts (and some comment on their audits) to some trustee or group of trustees. Where these are not the Board, the accounts are, of course, transmitted to them for approval. A few specific comments were:

'Once they have been approved by the Board, they are transmitted to the Regional Health Authority with the District Auditor's report. If the report and accounts suggest a major problem, the executives and non-executives may be liable to appear before the Public Accounts Committee.'

'There is no Audit Committee, but the partner-in-charge presents a report to the [Board] in person, together with the fully completed accounts.'

'There is an Audit Committee, which reports to the Finance Committee; it meets twice a year, once to consider the audited accounts, and again to consider the programme of work of the internal and external auditors. Members of the Management Board are present.'

'There is no Audit Committee at any level, but the Divisional Auditor usually attends the regional company meeting, at which he or she makes a personal report on the accounts.'

Management letter

Whether or not the auditor presents the accounts in person, there will usually be a formal letter sent to the client, setting out any weaknesses in the control systems, approaching problems and so on. The client is usually required to respond formally or at least to countersign the letter:

'Because this is a district audit, the audit certificate includes the material otherwise covered in a "management letter", and sets out action points for attention.'

'The auditors send a "management control letter" to the Finance Director, and this, together with the formal reply, is reviewed by the Audit Committee.'

'The auditors send a "management letter" to the Director or Finance Director as appropriate, but this is sometimes quite a brief document; it is not passed on to the trustees unless it contains something of note.'

'Individual "letters of management" are sent to the Director, the Deputy Director and the Treasurer, with a request for comment. Subsequent letters refer to the extent to which proposed amendments to the system or practice have been implemented, and have been effective.'

'The auditors send a "management letter" to the Chair, who sends it on to the Honorary Treasurer, and thence to the Audit Committee.'

'The auditors do not send a "management letter" to the trustees, as such. However, they do submit a "report" which covers some of the ground of such a document, including a breakdown, although it mostly consists of material which might more appropriately be part of the "Notes to the Accounts".'

'The auditors do not often submit "management letters" (in addition to their verbal reports to the regional companies) unless there is something of significance to report.'

Internal controls

We now turn to the internal systems of control within the charities, set out in Table 12.

Sources of information

The first three columns of Table 12 give some information about other sources on which trustees (especially non-executive trustees) might base their confidence that the finances of their charity were under control. All but one of the charities prepare annual budgets, often as part of a multi-year business plan, which is required in order to secure their core-funding. However, the document is not always transmitted in full (or maybe not at all) to the full Board of Trustees; this must cast doubt on the ability of those who are not also members of the Executive (or other) Committee to fulfil their duty to administer the charity:

'An annual budget is prepared by the Director of Finance over an extended period from October to January/February, and submitted to the Board for approval. The reason for the length of this process is that, in addition to consultations with colleagues and the special interest groups, a major part of the exercise is an extensive negotiation and planning exercise with the various fundholders and authorities who make up the "internal market" for the Trust's services.'

'Following discussion of "bids" with committees, and meetings between individual committee chairs, the treasurers, the Chief Executive and the Chief Accountant, an annual budget is prepared by the Chief Executive and the Chief Accountant in November. [It is] discussed and approved by both the Finance Committee and the Executive Committee.'

'The Director of Finance prepares the charity's medium-term plan, which includes a rolling three-year financial plan. An annual budget, which derives from the plan, goes first to the Management Board and thence to the Finance Committee and Council.'

'The Finance Director prepares the charity's annual budget, based on a figure of "standard income" (this is a sustainable dividend/capital gain figure, agreed with the charity's investment managers).The budget is annual, and takes account of designated funds for future periods.'

'Although the charity aims to prepare a five-year plan in due course, currently only an annual plan is prepared by the Director of Finance, and approved by Council.'

TABLE 12 CONTROL SYSTEM IN OPERATION WITHIN THE CHARITY

Charity	Budget seen by	Management accounts prepared	Management accounts seen by	Formal control system
1	Board	Monthly	Clinical Directors and the Board	Yes and approved
2	Board	6-monthly	Board	No
3	Finance Committee and Executive Committee	Monthly	Finance Committee	Yes
4	Finance Committee and Board	Monthly	Finance Committee; relevant sections to other committee chairs	Yes
5	Executive Committee	3-monthly	Board; relevant sections to subcommittees	Yes and approved
6	Executive Committee and Board	Monthly	Senior management team; Executive Committee; summary to Board	Yes
7	Executive Committee	3-monthly	Executive Committee; Board	No
8	Board	2-monthly	Finance Committee; Board	Yes
9	Finance Committee and Board	3-monthly	Chief Executive; key figures and extracts to Finance Committee	Yes and approved
10	Board	None	N/A	No
11	Executive Committee and Board	Monthly	Executive Committee	No
12	Executive Committee	Monthly	Chair of Trustees; Finance Committee; relevant sections to other committees; quarterly summaries to Executive Committee	No
13	Board	Monthly	Directors and heads of departments	No
14	Board	Monthly	Senior management team; Board	Yes
15	Executive Committee	Monthly	Executive Committee	No
16	Finance Committee and Board	3-monthly	Finance Committee; Executive Committee; appropriate sections to heads of departments	Yes
17	Policy and Resources Committee and Board	Monthly	Chief Executive; Policy and Resources Committee; Board	Yes
18	Bursars and Headmasters	Termly	Governors; consolidated versions to regional committees	Yes

Comparison with budget

All our respondents, save one, prepare regular management accounts, which always contain comparisons with budget figures. A major part of the control exercised over financial matters by the trustees must be their ability to review these figures and demand explanations of any variances. To the extent that the management accounts also show the cumulative actual performances against budget, the final period's management accounts also provide a monitored version of the figures on which the final published accounts should be based.

'The Chief Accountant also prepares monthly management accounts, which go to all members of the Finance Committee, together with a commentary by the Chief Executive.'

'The Finance Division prepares monthly management accounts, which go to the senior management team and, on a quarterly basis, to the Executive Committee, with a summary to the full Board of Trustees. Monthly accounts are also prepared for the trading subsidiaries, and these go to the respective boards, also on a quarterly basis.'

'The Director of Finance also prepares quarterly management accounts, on the basis of returns from regional offices, which are sent to the Director General. Key figures are made available to the Finance Committee at each meeting, with extracts from quarterly accounts as they appear.'

'Neither cash forecasts nor interim management accounts are prepared. The comparatively stable and long-term nature of the Foundation's activities make it useful to adopt an "actuarial" view of its financial situation – much as in the case of a pension fund.'

'An income and expenditure report is prepared each month for use by the Budgetary Control Committee and Council . . . The Director of Finance provides detailed departmental budget reports for directors and heads of department.'

Procedures

Whilst all the respondent charities *do* have systems of control in place, these are not always enshrined in a formal document. There may be managerial reasons for making 'control' a more or a less flexible matter, but the advantage of a formal Manual of Procedures is that copies can be given to trustees, who can therefore consider exactly how things are supposed to be run. In some cases, the informality of the system would appear to be compensated by remarkably low limits on what can be ordered or paid for without the signature of a trustee – but this is not always the case.

'There is no formal document setting out the protocols for placing of orders, cash control, the appointment and dismissal of junior staff and the appointment of suppliers and the like. The matter is not the subject of much discussion by the trustees – nor of enquiry by the external auditor. Nevertheless, the full-time officers have inherited a most elaborate body of "oral tradition" about these matters, especially with respect to handling cash. These appear to be based on local government procedures, and to have been commended to the charity at its inception!'

'There is no specific manual setting out the system of internal control. The placing of orders, cash control (etc) are undertaken by staff members, within fairly tight limits. All expenditure over £200 requires the signature of one or more trustees.'

'The operations take place under the general authority of the Director, and by custom the four senior members of staff have authority for signing cheques up to £10,000; thereafter the signature of a trustee is also required. As for receipts, it should be appreciated that the major items are received by direct credit to the Foundation's bank account; in general, the Foundation's staff is considered too small to justify elaborate divisions of duty for security-check reasons.'

'The Administrator receives and banks cash and cheques, and reconciles the cashbook with the bank statements. She and the Director of Care Services can jointly sign cheques up to the value of £500; those for larger amounts are signed by the Chair.'

'There is no single, formal document setting out the protocols . . . However, the charity has a very definite structure of control over these matters, which defines both levels of authority and demarcations of authority. These attach to the various grades of staff within the charity, and are reviewed by the Finance Committee from time to time. It occasionally happens that some post requires, for example, different levels from those of its specific grade; these are negotiated with the Finance Director by the senior staff concerned with the post. These procedures refer to comparatively routine items, and the trustees may be considered to control them through the budgetary system. However, this charity undertakes major capital expenditure as part of the normal budget, and these items are specifically authorised and monitored by the trustees in considerable detail.'

'The procedures for dealing with cash, orders, cheques and so on are derived through experience, and subject to annual audit.'

'The placing of orders (etc) takes place under the general authority of the Head of Finance, subject to a detailed protocol of cash limits etc. The appointment and dismissal of all staff take place under the general authority of [the Chief Executive]; there are now tight controls on the filling of any post.'

'The protocols for dealing with cash, orders, cheques and so on are set out, in a general way, in the rules and bye-laws of each school. These are occasionally reviewed by the fellows.'

Narrative report

Because charity accounts are notoriously difficult to interpret, the law, recommended practice and custom dictate that every charity should prepare an annual *narrative* report to accompany its accounts. The 'official line' is that this should be single report, signed on behalf of the trustees as a body, but general practice still seems to prefer a series of personal reports from various individuals. The situation is complicated by the fact that many charities are companies-limited-by-guarantee, which are thought to require a very formal (and sparse!) form of report; this is often prepared and presented quite separately from the full report.

TABLE 13 WHO PRESENTS THE REPORTS?

Charity	'Full' report presented by	'Company's' report presented by
1	Under review	N/A
2	Chair and officers	Auditor
3	None	CEO/Auditor/Treasurer
4	CEO	Auditor
5	Officers	Auditor
6	Finance Director	N/A
7	None?	CEO
8	PR Department	Auditor
9	Officers	N/A
10	Staff	N/A
11	None	Auditor
12	Staff	N/A
13	PR and Education Department	Auditors
14	Director of Public Affairs	Auditor
15	CEO	N/A
16	Secretary to Council	N/A
17	Head of Marketing	Head of Finance and Committee Clerk
18	Officers	Auditors

? not clear from interview

Table 13 sets out who seems to be the *principal* author(s) of these two reports. The occasional references to 'PR', 'Publicity' etc for the full report and the much more frequent 'Auditor' for the company version suggest what is probably the perceived purpose of the two documents in most cases. Both are rather removed from the intention of the 'official line' in the Charities SORP, which seeks to provide further insights into the specific content of the *accounts*. The following quotes show how some of our respondents go about it.

'The narrative reports included with the published Annual Report include individual statements from the Chairman, the Director and the Treasurer. These are prepared by appropriate members of staff, in consultation with the person in question, and accompany the audited accounts through the cycle of discussion and approval . . . However, the Report also includes much more general narrative and statistical material. This is prepared by the appropriate staff, and approved by three trustees, but does not go before the Executive Committee for more formal approval.'

'The narrative reports included with the Annual Report are prepared jointly by the Public Relations Department and the Education Department, from input by appropriate members of staff. The result is forwarded to the Director General, and it is finally scrutinised by the senior officers. The narrative report is not directly approved by Council.'

'The Director of Public Affairs prepares a framework in April, which goes to the Director General; the final text is prepared by the Publications Department, in consultation with the relevant departmental directors.'

'Around about February, the Secretary to the Council asks the various heads of department for material to be included in the annual narrative report. At about the same time, the Director of Press and Publicity is extracting suitable items from the narrative reports of the branches. This material is then worked up by the Director of Press and Publicity into the report submitted to the Secretary to the Council, the Controller and the Chairman of Trustees, and subsequently to Council for approval.'

'The narrative reports are assembled in the same way [as the accounts]. Those at regional level are prepared by the regional bursar and the regional chair.'

We observed in Chapter 1 that it is not easy to audit the content of these narrative sections of the annual financial report in the absence of a formal system of monitoring the field activities of the charity. Some may dispute whether monitoring the actual charitable activities is a proper part of its financial governance. A traditional view might be that the trustees were non-executives concerned with fundraising and doling out the proceeds to the applicants or internal departments etc who make calls upon them. Perhaps that is something taken care of through the system of budgetary control.

It is necessary, however, to bear in mind that the financial transactions of a charity have little obvious significance; there are no benchmarks such as net profit or return on investment. If trustees cannot or do not monitor the fieldwork itself, the budget process is reduced to a paperwork square-dance. Moreover, in the absence of a formal, verifiable flow of information about work in the field, the detailed Trustees' Report recommended by the Charities SORP can never be more than a collection of anecdotes. Here is how some of our respondent charities conduct their business:

'The healthcare operations of the hospital are dealt with under the supervision of the Medical Director and the Chief Nurse/Head of Operations . . . They report to the Board in the first instance, and also to the appropriate Special Interest Group(s); the form and method of collating their formal narrative reports is currently under discussion. "Applications for assistance" to an NHS trust take the form of referrals from fundholding GPs and Health Authorities. They are unusual . . . to the extent that these referrals also provide the "donations" that form a major part of the Trust's income. Extensive records are kept with respect to patient care, much of it in formats that have been devised externally . . . '

'The charitable operations of this charity are handled primarily by staff under the control of the Director of Housing Services, who reports to the Housing Management Committee . . . New applicants fill out an application form and are visited at home. Their applications and the reports of the visitors are evaluated in terms of an established Housing Services Policy, so that their housing need can be assessed.'

'Land, buildings and chattels are acquired by the charity, either by purchase or by donation. The charity assesses all proposed acquisitions using established "merit" criteria. The charity's ownership of properties is permanent, because it declares most of its properties inalienable. Thus, new properties must be "endowed" by setting aside funds for their maintenance . . .'

'The machinery for the Foundation's operations is fairly self-evident from the committee structure that deals with them. Department staff process applications, obtain assessments and monitor the progress of grants and projects . . . The question of monitoring such projects is difficult, especially with respect to single, one-off projects. It may be easier to measure overall achievement, where a group of projects can be seen as a "scheme" with some specific theme. It has been suggested that some more sophisticated set of criteria should be developed. However, the trustees feel this to be undesirable, in a general way; researchers may be tempted to devote more time to fulfilling criteria than to scientific advancement . . .'

'The Director of Care services . . . makes a monthly report to the Executive Committee and contributions to newsletters; there is no formal annual report on the charitable operations . . . Flyers are distributed to local doctors and hospitals, outlining the services available through the charity. Case notes are prepared for all applicants . . . All applicants are seen by a volunteer doctor. The case notes are monitored by the Director of Care Services, and form the basis of her reports to the Executive Committee . . .'

'The on-going activities of the charity are largely controlled at the branch and regional levels, and calls for assistance are dealt with there. There are criteria for identifying major incidents which [the security forces] are required to report additionally and immediately to the charity's headquarters control-room. Other incidents are reported by the [local branch] on a regular basis.'

'The existence of the five regional offices means that there is rarely a need to open up a new area to the charity's work . . . The regional managers' monthly reports alert the charity to any probable worsening of the situation in their regions, and the steps needed to relieve it. There is close liaison between these offices and the Fundraising Department, since a fair proportion of the charity's public appeals (for better or worse) have to be linked to public concern created by news reports of disasters.'

'The charitable operations of a university are handled by the appropriate schools and faculties, reporting to the Academic Board . . . It is the reports of the faculties that form the basis of the university's overall narrative report. In general, applications from would-be students are dealt with by the well-known multiple-applications and clearing-house system . . . Extensive records are kept of student applications, examinations and general academic progress. The "case notes" are monitored by the appropriate academic departments, and form some part of the basis for reports to the Academic Board.'

Other issues

Three further issues of financial control are worthy of comment: they concern computers, transactions involving foreign currencies and cash flow.

Computers

Almost all our respondent charities operate computer systems of some sort, for accounting and statistical/database purposes. Given the comparatively high average age of many Boards of Trustees, one might suppose that their understanding of information technology and computer-security matters may not be substantial. There follows a sample of what is said about these matters:

'The accounting and statistical records of the Trust are maintained on a computer, which is operated under the control of the Director of Finance; there is a back-up file system and the trust is in the course of making an appointment of an information-technology specialist. The Chief Executive has moderate experience of computing matters. Several non-executive members of the Board of Trustees also have some experience with information technology, from their service as hospital administrators or their own business activities.'

'There is a small in-house computer system, handling payroll, sales invoicing and the preparation of remittance advices. Cheques are hand-written, and the cashbooks are also maintained manually. The equipment is operated by the full-time staff, who also write up the other books. The external auditor does not enquire about computer matters on a regular basis.'

'The accounting records are maintained on a computer, which is operated by a specialist computer manager; there is a back-up file system. The system is currently the subject of review by a firm of consultants, but the absence of much computer knowledge among the other executives and trustees is not seen as a major problem here.'

'There is no computer security officer as such, but Internal Audit has a responsibility in this area, as has the Housing Corporation inspectorate. The trustees do not appear to have any great appreciation of the issues involved in computer security.'

'The auditors have a double responsibility in the case of the banking subsidiary, as they report on its "systems" to the Bank of England. As for the trustees, their extensive involvement with banking, for example, means that many have a good appreciation of the issues involved in computer security.'

'There is also a specialist Computer Auditor, and an Internal Procedures Manual for the system. In addition there is a PC network, covering regional offices and key properties. There is a specialist Information Technology Department. The Director of Finance has a moderate understanding of information technology, but it is doubtful whether any of the trustees is especially knowledgeable in such matters.'

'There is no in-house computer system, although payroll and a number of other routine tasks are performed by a bureau . . .'

'In-house computer security depends on levels of access, controlled by passwords, plus normal back-up, manuals etc. However, the auditors take a very substantial interest in these issues. The Finance Committee oversees computer policy and has a computer expert as one of its members.'

'There is an Information Technology Officer, whilst systems security and back-up are dealt with by a specialist firm. None of the trustees has received a detailed briefing on issues involved in computer security.'

'Each school decides on its own accounting/statistical record-keeping; some have computers, others use bureaux, others are entirely manual.'

Foreign currency transactions

Issues concerning foreign exchange and money market deposits have recently been controversial. Several of our sample of charities have extensive transactions in other currencies, but they rarely seem to give cause for concern.

'The charity has extensive transactions in foreign currencies and actually maintains bank balances in some of them. However, the transactions do not involve covering trading transactions, so no hedging is involved in their operation.'

'A small proportion of its income and expenditure is in Irish punts, but this is not a great problem to the extent that orders, deliveries and payments are not subject to long delays. However, the charity is now buying substantial items from Germany, where substantial losses and gains on conversion may be possible. The Finance Standing Committee is currently giving consideration to the possibility of hedging these transactions.'

'The charity has considerable foreign transactions with respect to the Ministry of Defence contract, but the financial arrangements for these are handled by the Ministry itself.'

Cash flow

Many charities suffer from somewhat 'lumpy' cash flows, making it necessary to carry large cash balances at certain times. These are sometimes invested on the money market, usually through firms of investment managers who may also handle the charities' other investments as well.

'There are some very limited endowment investments, handled by brokers, who report to the divisional chapters. For the most part, the schools' finances involve careful management of an overdraft/balance on current account, throughout the year.'

'There are specific policies for dealing with investments, including cash deposits, through firms of brokers and the charity's bankers. These arrangements are under the supervision of the Investment Subcommittee.'

'The charity's cash deposits are dealt with by the Finance Department in accordance with a policy laid down by Council, which includes the names of approved deposit-takers. Investments are managed by a firm of stockbrokers, who report to an Investment Advisory Group consisting of trustees and a number of co-opted specialists.'

'There are investments to be made on the money markets. These are handled by investment managers under the delegated authority of the Investment Committee, within parameters laid down by Council. Investment in certain companies is prohibited on ethical grounds . . .'

'. . . the charity's Charter lays down the rules for its investments in some detail. The major investments are handled by brokers within those rules. There are some limited direct investments of cash, under strict guidelines, with named AAA deposit-takers.'

'Money is deposited with prime banks, commonly Barclays; there is no list of approved deposit-takers, however.'

'The cash deposits of the charity and its subsidiaries are dealt with on advice from a firm of brokers, acting within the Large Exposure Rules of the Bank of England in the case of the banking subsidiary . . .'

'The charity has a deposit account at a building society – and no other investments. Questions of security of this item, or any concept of approved deposit-takers, do not seem to concern the trustees!'

Summary and issues

The most noticeable feature of Table 10 is that no fewer than fifteen of our sample are audited by large or very large firms. It might seem that our sample is biased toward large or very large charities, but this is not the case. In fact, our impression has been that a good many of our respondents are considerably 'over-engined' in this respect.

A possible explanation of this phenomenon can be seen from their lengths of service. Nine of those firms have served for from 20-odd years to 'time out of mind', during which many local firms have merged into the present larger units. Another feature also explains at least two examples of possible over-engining: the firms in question also acted for the founder of the charity.

One charity has a policy of putting its audit out to tender on a five-year cycle and another is thinking of adopting this policy. Several more claim that the reappointments are not automatic, whilst one makes the useful point that they regularly revise the auditors' terms of engagement to take account of changes in their systems. However, some are more forthright in extolling the virtues of continuity. For example:

'Now that a top-ranking firm has been appointed, covering the charity's work at home and abroad, it is expected that it will remain in office for many years, subject to periodic review by the Audit Committee.'

As befits its federal nature, Charity 18 makes use of many firms of auditors:

'Auditors exist at all three levels of the charity's administration. They are all paid for their work, are local practitioners in the area of the school/division, and are registered auditors. They rarely change: any changes are usually the result of a change in the geographical "centre" of a division, following a reorganisation. In some cases, the school's auditors also prepare the accounts.'

The data in Table 11 are largely self-explanatory; however, as the comments of the trustees have shown, the messages do not always get through. The auditors usually hold a formal 'final meeting' of some sort with the Chief Executive, Finance Director and so on at the conclusion of their audits. However, some also have a meeting with the Treasurer (or some other trustee(s)), prior to the presentation of the audited accounts to the Audit Committee or some other committee of trustees. This is probably helpful, especially if the committee in question is rather large and the more technical difficulties can be explained fully. The disadvantage may be the reinforcement of a natural tendency for the other, less involved, trustees to suppose that, if the Honorary Treasurer (and thereafter the Audit Committee, the Finance Committee and the Executive Committee) is happy, all must be well.

'The audited accounts are initially considered by the Treasurer and his deputy, in a meeting with the auditor. They are immediately transmitted (with some part of the narrative report) to the Finance . . . Committee.'

As we have shown, some of our respondents are subject to a considerable amount of auditing and inspection, from more than one source. In some cases the various agencies do not get together to discuss their programmes of work or their findings. Not only may this involve expensive duplication of activity, it is equally possible that some areas may be omitted from any testing – and weaknesses detected by one group may not be observed by the others.

'The Trust is audited by the District Auditor. The trustee feels that this quite costly matter could be dealt with most effectively if the District Auditor evaluated the work of the Trust's own Internal Audit Section, and allowed the bulk of the compliance testing to be dealt with by the internal audit (at a substantially lower cost to the Trust).'

'The Head of Internal Audit plays a major role in servicing [the Audit Committee, and] has direct access to the Executive Director and the Audit Committee itself, if need be . . . The auditors have, to date, had no formal communication with the Head of Internal Audit, but at the charity's request, they review the programme of work of her department.'

'The auditors also have formal communication with the Head of Internal Audit, through attendance at meetings of the Audit Committee, where they participate in the review of the internal audit programme. The external auditors receive copies of all internal audit reports.'

Current ideas about financial governance revolve around the appointment of audit committees, consisting of non-executives, who will communicate with the external auditor in the absence of any executives. Our sample contains a number of audit committees but they rarely exclude executive trustees and paid executives are commonly present. We have recorded comments as to the impossibility of either holding conversations with auditors without expert interpretation or of a non-executive being able to reach any conclusions about the accounts independently of the executives. On the face of it, this aspect of financial governance of charities is in a poor state.

However, if one steps back from this concentration on the audit committee and considers the data in Table 12, the position is much brighter. Most of our respondents have long-term business plans, and all but one have budgets and regular management accounting statements produced to a substantial number of executive and non-executive trustees. The plans and budgets are commonly related to a formal mission statement of the charity's objectives. It is clear that most trustees *do* read and understand these documents and pursue variances from plan in some detail; moreover, the management accounts are accumulated throughout the year, so the final period's cumulative figures should form the basis for the final audited financial report.

Possible sources of weakness might be the absence of clear machinery either for acquainting the auditor with the minuted questions and replies on variances from budget or for ensuring that the non-executive trustees really understand any adjustments between the cumulative management accounts and the published accounts. It would seem that it is the arcane curiosities of the latter that defeat most trustees; it may be unfortunate that the current drive for greater accounting *disclosure* tends to make those accounts more baffling still.

All our respondent charities have systems for the control of cash and accounting in general, including computer security. This is almost always in written form but is rarely the subject of line-by-line consideration by the non-executive (or executive!) trustees. Not many of the charities have any formal internal audit department to check on the compliance with these systems but a surprising number are subject to external inspections of all or part of their systems by other bodies – and ad hoc inspections by senior members of staff, executive trustees and consultants are also fairly common. A possible weakness is a failure to co-ordinate the findings of these various compliance inspections or to communicate them to the external auditor and non-executive trustees.

A narrative report is needed to give any sort of meaning to the financial figures. In general, the situation revealed by Table 13 and the material relating to it is less than good, if only because so few charities truly conform with the spirit of the Charities SORP: they do not produce a comprehensive, rigorous analysis of their activities and their relationship to the accounting record – signed on behalf of the trustees as a body. Instead, they continue to produce personal statements from individuals plus unashamedly PR-based material of a general nature.

The weakness is that this approach is basically *anecdotal* and the resulting narratives can neither readily be checked against any source documents nor shown to be comprehensive statements of what has occurred. In fact, the remedy is already at hand for most of our respondents, provided that they have maintained adequate minutes of the discussions arising from the setting of their budgets, including the comparison of their management accounts with that budget. These must provide the material for exactly the commentary recommended in the SORP, in a comprehensive and checkable form.

It would seem to be essential that every non-executive trustee should take part in all these exercises. If they do not, it is hard to see how they can possibly be in a position to monitor the activities of the executive in the wider interests.

Finally, we need to consider what has been learned about the external audit of charities. Many auditors have been in post for very long periods and few charities have any real policy for considering their replacement. In general, their letters of engagement are rather old, if not lost in time! Charities seem often to be 'over-engined' in their auditors, but this may reflect the probable lack of specialist knowledge in smaller, generalist firms. This no doubt also explains the reluctance to change auditors once an appointment has been made.

External auditors commonly attend to explain the results of their audit to the trustees, with varying degrees of mutual comprehension; it may be that they do not sufficiently involve the *executive* trustees (as opposed to the paid officials) in their 'audit queries' in the course of their work. In general, the trustees seem satisfied with the auditors' activities; the more informed trustees have reasonably sensible expectations of the audit process, but the less knowledgeable give plenty of evidence of the so-called 'audit expectations gap'.

POINTS FOR DISCUSSION

10a Whether a charity should always have an audit committee, consisting of all of the non-executive trustees.

10b Whether that committee should meet at least twice a year, with the external auditor in attendance, but with no other trustees or paid officials present except for a minute-secretary.

10c Whether one meeting should consider the various compliance reports on the charity's system, and establish the auditor's programme of work in the light of these reports.

10d Whether the audit committee should meet on another occasion to consider the audited accounts, together with a detailed analysis of any adjustments made to the cumulative management accounts, and the auditor's 'management letter' or other commentary on the audit or the accounts, prior to their submission to the Board or Council for approval.

10e Whether, at least once in every three years, the committee should consider the detail of the charity's financial control systems, and invite the auditor's comments thereon.

10f Whether, at least once in every three years, the committee ought to reconsider the terms of the auditor's letter of engagement.

10g Whether every charity should prepare at least an annual budget, which should be approved by the full Board of Trustees.

10h Whether, at least once a quarter, all members of the Board of Trustees should receive a set of cumulative management accounts, setting out variances with the budget, and proper minutes should be kept of any comments thereon and the explanations put forward to explain any variances.

10i Whether every charity should prepare a formal trustees' report on behalf of the whole Board of Trustees, that complies fully with the spirit of the charities SORP.

10j Whether the audit committee should formally consider the adequacy of this report, in the light of the minutes of the Board of Trustees, before its submission to the Board or Council for approval.

10k Whether the professional bodies of accountants should be urged to include more material on both voluntary sector accounting and auditing *and* communication skills in their examination syllabuses and requirements for practical experience.

There was one aspect of financial governance about which we confined our questions to the trustees rather than the executives of our respondent charities. This related to the policy on reserves. The Charity Commission has issued draft guidelines on this matter and the NCVO has set up an associated working party.

On the matter of what a charity's policy toward the creation of reserves of funds should be, the trustees can best be left to speak for themselves.

'Although the Charity Commission urges trustees to fully expend their funds, basic requirements of prudence require a charity to build up some reserves "against a rainy day". He has no theoretical basis for calculating a suitable amount, but believes that they should be "substantial" in the case of this charity, because its "enabling charity" activities mean that most of its expenditures are fixed . . .'

'The issue is complicated, in the case of the Foundation, by the fact that it has no permanent endowment, and would appear to be at liberty to spend its capital . . .'

'Charities should be encouraged to spend their resources to the full, subject to the need to make proper provision for repairs and other longer term liabilities.'

'The question of building and maintaining reserves is the second most important aspect of financial management in a charity. Nevertheless, it is difficult to arrive at a logical calculation . . . This charity tries to retain no less than two to two and a half times its annual expenditure; this can probably be justified by its unconditional commitment to the governments of the UK and Ireland to maintain an efficient service, involving a committed substantial capital investment plan . . .'

'. . . this charity currently has reserves equal to about 15% of its annual income, but a considerably higher figure would be preferable, in view of this charity's obligations in respect of existing properties and possible acquisitions.'

'This charity has a policy of seeking to retain, in liquid funds, an amount equal to about one-half its budgeted expenditure for the year. This is because it is highly dependent on legacies for its income . . .'

'This charity has been notably short of funds in recent years! However, the trustee believes that, ideally, a charity should hold in reserve between 3% and 5% of its average annual income. This appears to be the bench-mark for schools and educational establishments in general.'

'An NHS trust cannot really have any reserves at all; they are supposed to break even on a cash basis annually.'

'The charity is heavily dependent on foreign visitors, so events such as Lockerbie and Chernobyl can "decimate" its income overnight. It is therefore necessary to retain highly liquid reserves, equivalent to one whole year's income, to ensure the charity's survival in a disaster scenario.'

'. . . In his view, his own charity seems to plan its activities somewhat within its expected income – and take the balance to reserves.'

In short, not one of our respondents could produce a truly defensible calculation for their reserve policies! Large proportions and even multiples of annual expenditure are taken out of thin air, or else small surpluses are squirreled away 'against a rainy day'. There can be no doubt that *some* charities need reserve funds. 'Budget financed' charities differ from similarly financed local and central government because they rely on voluntary support rather than on enforceable tax demands. Self-financing not-for-profit businesses have less, if any, need for reserves and in general these charities do not have them.

In our view, proper calculations would not be difficult to prepare. The technique of 'flexible budgeting' would solve the problem. What charities currently call their budgets are in reality their 'most likely budgets'; they should, and many no doubt do, consider what would happen if circumstances turned out somewhat differently. The 'reserves' should be the sum necessary to make good the shortfall of income under a budget for 'the Doomsday scenario', when everything that can go wrong, does. Once calculated, it might be appropriate to set the amount aside into a special contingency fund.

This exercise might encourage trustees to consider the real probability of the proposed Doomsday scenario – and perhaps settle for some more moderate catastrophe. Also, it might make it easier to identify those 'rainy days' when it becomes appropriate to draw down from the contingency fund.

POINTS FOR **DISCUSSION**

10l Whether charities should expend the whole of their income every year, subject to making provision for known long-term liabilities and any properly calculated reserves for the future.

10m Whether charities should adopt the technique of flexible budgeting and whether such a budget should always support any reserves of funds to be carried forward.

10n Whether any such reserves should be set aside into a designated contingency fund.

Broad conclusions

Over all, our research leads us to believe that the voluntary sector has reached a level of development at which the current, cumulative legal and fiscal arrangements can be made to conform to the reality of their situations only by most complex administrative machinery. It is possible that it is the complexities that give rise to apparent excessive regulation of the voluntary sector and excessive complications in its tax regime.

We hope that the cumulative effect of this research project and an ever-increasing body of studies in this area will be a major and fundamental reform of the whole corpus of legislation relating to voluntary organisations.

A basis for reform is, we suggest, proposals that have been made by the European Union for a European Association. It is necessary to understand that the concept of 'a charity' is exclusively British, and dates from the swift and complete Dissolution of the Monasteries in Tudor times! Much the same tasks are carried out by voluntary organisations elsewhere in the world but their organisation is subtly different in several respects. These differences are well summarised (at least for Europe) by the Draft Regulations for the European associations, which are currently before the Commission. These associations are intended to be the voluntary sector equivalent of the European company, and thus to have the status of officially registered charities throughout the Union. To be sure, these bodies are not likely to become very numerous, the legislation is not currently very near the top of any agenda at Brussels and the draft clearly needs more work, but we may assume that the draft is an informed digest of European procedures in the area (including the British ones). The principal features of the proposed associations are as follows.

■ They will be incorporated bodies with limited liability. British registered charities do not have limited liability, so an increasing number of charities are now choosing to register additionally as limited companies, usually as 'companies-limited-by-guarantee'. Twelve of our subjects are so registered, and, because a number are also in some sense 'registered' as NHS trusts, universities and housing associations, the trustees would seem to be wearing up to three hats at once! (In fact, doubt has been expressed by some respondents as to whether this simple ploy will truly work: unless the contract specifically names the company, it is hard to see how trustees of the charity itself could shelter behind it.)

- The Association will be formed for some public purpose. This seems broader than the definition of a charitable purpose, and could cover just those political and sporting activities that cause problems for British charities. Of course, the tax exemptions available to voluntary organisations vary in other parts of Europe, where the self-sacrificing element in voluntary service may be of less moment than in the UK.

- The Association may carry on trades, provided that any profits are not distributed to individuals. All but one of our respondent charities have one or more trading companies, which have had to be registered separately.

- They will have members, who will elect directors. The Regulations do not seem to inhibit payments to directors, nor prevent them from acting in an executive capacity.

- Indeed, the implication is rather that there *will* be executive directors. As befits a European body, an Association must have specific arrangements for the representation of its employees, and preferably a two-tier board. This might be less of anathema to British charities than to British business! Ten of our respondents have a number of trustees who are appointed by other bodies. In a few cases, these people are notably inactive, whilst others are said to be prone to see themselves as delegates acting on behalf of their sponsors rather than in the interest of the charity as a whole. An advisory board might more precisely capture what, in many cases, both the charities and the sponsoring bodies truly expect of these people. Moreover, it will be seen that many of our charities supplement their subcommittee membership with co-opted 'experts' of various types, who are not trustees at all; it might be desirable to afford these people a more visible position within the charity.

Were it possible to set up such 'associations' under British law, there would still be many issues relating to governance that would need to be determined. But, given that every charity in our sample has one or more companies, one must also reflect that a good deal of administrative effort might be saved if all charities were automatically created as corporations with limited liability and authority to trade on a not-for-profit basis. In addition, charities would not then be tempted to treat as side-issues the important work currently being carried on through these companies. It would also provide a 'one stop' method of setting up a voluntary organisation of any type, without the need for trading companies or companies-limited-by-guarantee in order to trade or to obtain the benefits of incorporation with limited liability.

However, it must be said that it is unlikely that anyone concerned with charity matters would view the European Association proposals without many reservations. As with the trustee structure and committee structure of any old-established charity, trustees and their advisers have, over the centuries, arrived at a series of understandings with the Courts, the Executive and the tax authorities, which work, albeit in a less than entirely satisfactory fashion. Any reform along such lines would have to confront these arrangements and considerable further research would be needed to assess the likely effects of any change.

Nevertheless, in our view the goal should be the possibility of registering an incorporated voluntary organisation with limited liability and the right to trade, together with a tax regime driven by a specific social policy toward such organisations.

Accounting Standards Committee (1988) *SORP 2: Accounting by Charities*, ASC, London.

Archbishops' Commission on Cathedrals (1994) *Heritage and Renewal*, Church House Publishing, London.

Charity Accounting Review Committee (1993) *Exposure Draft: SORP 2, Accounting by Charities*, CARC, London.

Charity Accounting Review Committee (1995) *Accounting by Charities*, Statement of Recommended Practice, CARC, London.

Commission of the European Communities (1992) *Proposal for a Council Regulation (EEC) on the Statute for a European Association* (COM [91] 273 final – SYN 386), CEC, Brussels.

Gambling T, R Jones and C Kunz (1993) *The Revision of SORP 2 (Accounting by Charities)*, Certified Research Report No 34, Chartered Association of Certified Accountants, London.

Gambling T, R Jones and R Karim (1993) 'Credible organizations: self-regulation v external standard-setting in Islamic banks and British charities', *Financial Accountability and Management*, Vol 9, No 3, August 1993, 195–207.

Gambling T, R Jones, C Kunz and M Pendlebury (1990) *Accounting by Charities: the Application of SORP 2*, Certified Research Report No 21, Chartered Association of Certified Accountants, London.

Home Office Voluntary Services Unit (1995) *Accounting by Charities: Draft Regulations*, Home Office Voluntary Services Unit, London. Final version *The Charities (Accounts and Reports) Regulations 1995*, SI 2724.

Knight, B (1993) *Voluntary Action*, Home Office, London.

National Council for Voluntary Organisations and Charity Commission Working Party (1992) *On Trust*, NCVO, London.

National Council for Voluntary Organisations and Charity Commission Working Party (1992) *Trustee Training and Support Needs*, NCVO, London.

Charity administration checklist

Preliminary

1   What percentage of the charity's income over the last three years comes from the following sources?

    Contracts with central/local government

    Other contracts

    Grants from central/local government

    Donations, legacies and other grants

    Dividends and interest

    Covenants from trading companies

    Other covenants

2   Is there any formal machinery in place to review (a) the effectiveness and (b) the cost-effectiveness of the charity's administrative procedures and controls? When were these last reviewed?

A Trustees

1   How many trustees are there?

2   How long has each of them served as trustee?

3   What consultation takes place before a new trustee is appointed?

4   How are the trustees elected or appointed?

5   How often can trustees be re-elected or reappointed?

6   What is said to new trustees about their responsibilities and legal liabilities?

7   What subcommittees of trustees exist? Who are their members? How are they appointed? What are the terms of reference of the subcommittees? How often do they report back to the main board of trustees?

8   Do trustees receive any remuneration, either directly or through connected companies or other bodies? Do they receive any expenses?

9   Have any of the trustees known family or business connections with other trustees?

10   Is there a policy of disclosing and minuting conflicts of interest? Do any trustees have a financial interest in, or receive remuneration from, a company, firm or other organisation which trades/which conducts business with the charity? What purchases or sales have occurred, over the last twelve months, between the charity and any of its trustees or employees?

11   How often do the trustees meet, either as a whole or in subcommittees? What is the quorum to make a valid meeting? What majority(ies) is needed to pass resolutions? How often has each member attended over the last twelve months?

12   Is there a formal meeting to approve the annual report and accounts? How many trustees attended that meeting? What steps are taken to acquaint absentees with the content of the report and accounts?

13   Who prepares the trustees' annual narrative report?

14   Who prepares the agenda for the meeting of the board of trustees and of any subcommittees? What regular reports are made to the main board by subcommittees? By officers? What arrangements exist for tabling large items of receipts or expenditure, or sensitive items of business?

15   Who prepares the minutes of the meetings of the main board of trustees, and of the subcommittees?

16   Have any trustees resigned during the last three years? What reasons did they give?

B Auditors

1   Are they paid or honorary? What qualifications do they possess? How long have they served?

2   How are the auditors appointed and reappointed? After what consultation(s)?

3   Is there an audit committee? What is its composition? How often does it meet? To whom does it report?

4 With whom do the auditors and their staff principally meet in the course of the audit? With whom do they clear any audit queries?

5 What is the wording of the audit certificate? Have the auditors qualified their report at any time in the last five years?

C Finance

1 When is the charity's year end? Who prepares the final accounts? What was the date on which the last set of accounts was approved by the trustees? What was the date of the audit certificate? What was the date on which the financial report was submitted to the Charity Commission?

2 Are any summarised accounts prepared? Who prepares them? What steps are taken to ensure that they are in accordance with the full accounts? To whom are they sent?

3 Is an annual budget prepared? By whom is it prepared, and who approves it? At what time of the year is this done? Are cash forecasts prepared? How often? When and by whom are they discussed and approved?

4 Are interim management accounts prepared? By whom and how often? Are the results compared with the budget, if any? To whom are they reported?

5 Who receives and banks the cash and cheques received? Who signs the cheques? What limits are placed on the size of cheques to be signed? How often is the cashbook reconciled with the bank statements, and by whom?

6 What is the machinery for authorising the acceptance of legacies and offers of donations? What is the machinery for approving payments to beneficiaries? How is the implementation of these decisions supervised?

7 Who approves the appointment and removal of suppliers to the charity? Who approves the engagement and dismissal of staff? What limits are placed on their personal authority in such matters? How and how often do they report back on such decisions?

8 Which trustees and members of staff have authority to place orders on behalf of the charity? Are these made or confirmed in writing? What limits exist on their personal authority in these matters?

9 Who passes the invoices for payment? Who approves the payment of creditors?

10 Who decides the insurance requirements of the charity? To whom are these issues reported? Is there a register of the fixed assets of the charity?

11 Is any part of the records of the charity maintained on a computer? Are there complete and up-to-date operating and systems manuals for the system? What back-up provisions and other security measures are in force to maintain the system's integrity? Which trustees or senior officers truly understand the system, apart from those immediately concerned with its operation?

12 Are any of the charity's transactions carried out in foreign currencies? Are the exposures to risks of losses covered by hedging operation in the currency market? What control mechanism exists to prevent abuse or unwise risk-taking in such matters?

13 What arrangements are made for the investment of surplus funds? Who vets the nomination of money-market deposit-takers? On what criteria? How are such decisions communicated to the main board of trustees? Are investments in stocks and shares managed by professional investment advisers?

14 Are investments in properties managed by professional agents? How, and how often, do these advisers and agents report to the trustees?

D Branches

1 What procedures exist for the creation or disbandment of branches of the charity? Are there a standard constitution and rules of procedure for such branches?

2 What autonomous branches does the charity have? What non-autonomous branches? Are they fundraising or spending charities?

3 What controls exist over their operations, particularly with respect to cash collections and collecting boxes?

4 What financial and other returns do they make? How often are these returns required? What was the maximum and the average delay experienced, during the last twelve months, in the receipt of these returns?

5 How often, and in what form, are the activities of branches made known to the trustees of the main charity?

E Members

1 Does the charity have members? Are there more than one class of member?

2 How are members appointed, selected or elected? What are the requirements for obtaining and continuing membership?

3 Are they beneficiaries of the charity? Do they undertake any responsibility for its debts?

4 Is there an annual general meeting of members? What powers does it have? Who draws up its agenda?

5 Are reports of previous AGMs, full financial statements or summarised accounts circulated to all members, whether they attend the AGM or not?

6 Do members receive a regular newsletter? If so, who prepares the material included as its contents?

F Staff

1 How many employees does the charity have, including those working in non-autonomous branches and in trading and other non-charity companies? How many are full-time employees? Are any of them remunerated wholly or partly by way of commission?

2 Who are its senior paid officers? What are their qualifications? How are their activities supervised? How are their salaries and conditions of employment determined? How long has the most senior officer been in post? What are the salary ranges of the senior people (by £5,000 'bands' over £30,000)?

3 Are all vacancies advertised? Who supervises the preparation and insertion of such advertisements?

4 How many voluntary workers are engaged, and what is the nature of their work?

5 Are any relatives of the trustees or senior officers also employed by the charity? What positions do they hold?

G Fundraising

1 Has the charity entered into any agreements with professional fundraisers during the last three years? What forms of contract have been used? How much has been paid to such people by way of fees and commissions?

2   Are any members of the charity's own staff engaged primarily in fundraising? What are their qualifications and/or experience for such work?

3   Do the staff and professional fundraisers comply with the codes of practice issued by the Institute of Charity Fundraising Managers? If not, what departures from the codes are permitted?

4   Has the charity permitted any commercial participator or other profit-seeking organisation to use its name or any symbol associated with the charity?

5   Has the charity, or any of its fundraisers, undertaken any solicitation of funds by direct mail? By telephone? Are there any instructions about the manner in which these solicitations should be made?

6   Has any appeal for funds been made on radio or television?

H   Non-charitable subsidiaries

1   Are there any such subsidiaries? How are they controlled? How frequently and to whom do these subsidiaries report on their activities? Do these reports include budgets and cash forecasts? How are these reports presented to the main board of trustees?

2   Do they operate from premises also used by the charity, or share any services of the charity's staff? If so, what arrangements exist as to rentals, etc or payment of wages?

3   How much has the charity invested in the subsidiaries? How much has the charity lent to the subsidiaries? Are these investments and loans permitted by the charity's governing instrument?

4   Are any of the trustees or members of the charity's staff also remunerated by any of the subsidiaries?

I   Charity Commission and other agencies

1   What queries have been addressed to the charity during the last three years by the Charity Commissioners, the Inland Revenue, Customs and Excise or any other agency of central or local government, either in the United Kingdom or elsewhere? Who has responded to them, and what was the outcome?

2   What steps are taken to ensure that the main board of trustees are aware of all such enquiries and their outcomes?

J Charitable operations

1 What is the organisation chart for the charitable operation(s)? Who is in overall charge? Who are his or her principal subordinates? What are their professional qualifications? To whom do the named personnel report? How often? Is an overall annual report of the charitable operations prepared? By whom? To whom is it circulated?

2 What external guidelines and codes of practice apply to the charitable operations? How is their observance monitored?

K Application for assistance and new projects

1 How is the availability of funds advertised (a) externally and (b) internally?

2 Are proper records kept of all applications for assistance, and how were these dealt with? Are proper case records kept in respect of external recipients of assistance? Are individual cost records kept for each internal project?

3 Are references taken up for external applicants? What supporting evidence for their projects is demanded from internal applicants?

4 How are the requests/proposals evaluated? By whom are beneficiaries/successful projects selected?

5 What follow-up is made of external applicants? How is the progress of internal projects reported?

6 By whom are these reports considered? Evaluated? How are they transmitted to the main board of trustees? How are they reflected in the trustees' annual report?

About CAF

CAF, Charities Aid Foundation, is a registered charity with a unique mission – to increase the substance of charity in the UK and overseas. It provides services that are both charitable and financial which help donors make the most of their giving and charities make the most of their resources.

Many of CAF's publications reflect the organisation's purpose: *Dimensions of the Voluntary Sector* offers the definitive financial overview of the sector, while the *Directory of Grant Making Trusts* provides the most comprehensive source of funding information available.

As an integral part of its activities, CAF works to raise standards of management in voluntary organisations. This includes grants made by its own Grants Council, sponsorship of the Charity Annual Report and Accounts Awards, seminars, training courses and the Charities' Annual Conference, the largest regular gathering of key people from within the voluntary sector. In addition, Charitynet is now established as the leading Internet site on voluntary action.

For decades, CAF has led the way in developing tax-effective services to donors and these are now used by more than 150,000 individuals and 2,000 of the UK's leading companies; many are also using CAF's CharityCard, the world's first debit card designed exclusively for charitable giving. For charities, CAF's unique range of investment and administration services includes the CafCash High Interest Cheque Account, two common investment funds for longer term investment and a full appeals and subscription management service.

However, CAF's activities are not limited to the UK and, increasingly, CAF is looking to apply the same principles and develop similar services internationally, in its drive to increase the substance of charity across the world.

About the ICAEW Research Board

The Research Board is the leading private sector sponsor of accounting research in the UK, with around £400,000 available for research grants and conferences in 1996. The Board aims to promote independent academic research of the highest quality, primarily within UK universities. The Board's policy is to concentrate its research efforts in areas that are central to the work of chartered accountants. The Research Strategy sets out the areas in which the Board is primarily concerned to concentrate its research programme. However, applications in respect of any original research ideas in accountancy and related fields are always welcome. Grants are available to researchers who are not Institute members.

The Board disseminates the results of its sponsored research as widely as possible amongst academics, practitioners, policy makers and the business community. All research must therefore be of publishable quality. In addition to seeking publication in refereed journals for its sponsored projects, the Board also publishes a series of refereed Research Monographs and each year enters into a number of agreements to publish hardback books in association with commercial publishers. A summary of the Board's activities is given in *Research Board News* which is published three times a year and sent to all university departments and to individuals who request it.

Anyone wishing to obtain a copy of the Research Strategy or other Research Board publications, or to receive *Research Board News*, should contact Jacqui Modeste at the Research Board, The Institute of Chartered Accountants in England and Wales, PO Box 433, Moorgate Place, London EC2P 2BJ. Enquiries relating to research grants should be directed to Jan Latham, Research Manager, at the same address. Telephone: 0171-920 8419.

About the CIMA Research Foundation
Providing relevant, recent research for management accounting

Chartered Institute of Management Accountants (CIMA) is the leading professional body for management accountants with membership of 42,000 chartered management accountants and 58,000 students worldwide. The aim of the CIMA Research Foundation is to promote the science of management accountancy by commissioning high-quality research to meet the needs of practising CIMA members.

As well as access to relevant, current research, the Research Foundation also provides a meeting ground for members to learn about new developments in theory and their use in practice. Members also have the opportunity to be regularly informed on research findings, ongoing projects and worldwide research conferences.

The Research Foundation also extends such information to non-CIMA members through the Financial Executives' Network (FE[n]). Details of this special subscription service can be obtained by calling + 44 (0) 171-580 2491.

If you would like further details about the other projects commissioned under the management information for trustees initiative or would like to learn more about the work of the Foundation, please contact + 44 (0) 171-917 9220.

A CIMA publications catalogue, which highlights CIMA's other research publications, can be sent to you free of charge if you call + 44 (0) 171-917 9277.

Index